Creating Healthy Work Organizations

WILEY SERIES IN WORK, WELL-BEING AND STRESS

Series Editor

CARY L. COOPER

Manchester School of Management
University of Manchester Institute of Science and
Technology, UK

Creating Healthy Work Organizations
Edited by Cary L. Cooper and Stephen Williams

Further titles in preparation

Creating Healthy Work Organizations

Edited by

CARY L. COOPER

Manchester School of Management,
University of Manchester Institute of Science and Technology, UK

and

STEPHEN WILLIAMS

Resource Assessment and Development, Harrogate, UK

with a Foreword by

JOHN BOWIS, MP

Parliamentary Under Secretary of State for Health

JOHN WILEY & SONS

Chichester · New York · Brisbane · Toronto · Singapore

658·382   AG   206056

Other Wiley Editorial Offices

John Wiley & Sons, Inc., 605 Third Avenue,
New York, NY 10158-0012, USA

Jacaranda Wiley Ltd, 33 Park Road, Milton,
Queensland 4064, Australia

John Wiley & Sons (Canada) Ltd, 22 Worcester Road,
Rexdale, Ontario M9W 1L1, Canada

John Wiley & Sons (SEA) Pte Ltd, 37 Jalan Pemimpin #05-04,
Block B, Union Industrial Building, Singapore 2057

Library of Congress Cataloging-in-Publication Data

Creating healthy work organizations / edited by Cary L. Cooper and
    Stephen Williams.
        p. cm. — (Wiley series in work, well-being, and stress)
    Includes bibliographical references and index.
    ISBN 0-471-94345-2 (cloth)
    1. Job stress. 2. Industrial hygiene. 3. Industrial safety.
    4. Work environment. 5. Work—Psychological aspects. I. Cooper,
    Cary L. II. Williams, Stephen, *1950–* . III. Series.
    HF5548.85.C74 1994   94–2441
    658.3'82—dc20   CIP

British Library Cataloguing in Publication Data

A catalogue record for this book is available from the British Library

ISBN 0-471-94345-2

Typeset in 11/13 pt Palatino by
Mathematical Composition Setters Ltd, Salisbury
Printed and bound in Great Britain by Biddles Ltd, Guildford, Surrey

Contents

Contributors

Cary L. Cooper
Editor

Professor of Organizational Psychology, Manchester School of Management, University of Manchester Institute of Science and Technology, PO Box 88, Manchester, M60 1QD.

Stephen Williams
Editor

Management Consultant, Resource Assessment and Development, Claro Court, Claro Road, Harrogate, HG1 4BA.

David C. Batman

Group Chief Medical Officer, Nestlé UK Ltd, York, YO1 1XY.

David Bunce

Research Psychologist, MRC/ESRC Social and Applied Psychology Unit, Department of Psychology, University of Sheffield, Sheffield, S10 2TN.

Ann Fingret

Consultant Physician in Charge of Occupational Medicine, Royal Marsden Hospital, London and Surrey, Fulham Road, London, SW3 6JJ. (Formerly Chief Medical Officer, BBC.)

Jeffrey A. Gray   Professor of Psychology and Head of Department, The Maudsley Hospital and The Institute of Psychiatry, De Crespigny Park, Denmark Hill, London, SE5 8AF.

Chris M. Judge   Human Resource Manager, Northern Telecom, Wireless Systems, 2920 Matheson Boulevard East, Mississauga, Ontario L4W 4M7, Canada.

Peter Leakey   Consultant Clinical Psychologist, Department of Clinical Psychology, North Derbyshire Health Authority, Walton Hospital, Chesterfield, Derbyshire.

Chuly Lee   Research Fellow, 36 Fortuna Court, 25 Repulse Bay Road, Hong Kong.

Mathew Littlewood   Consultant Clinical Psychologist, Derbyshire Dale Community Mental Health Team, Department of Clinical Psychology, North Derbyshire Health Authority, Dale Road, Matlock, Derbyshire, DE4 3LU.

Steve P. McKeown   Consultant Psychiatrist to ICI/Zeneca, UK President of the International Stress Management Association, Priory Therapy Centres, Masters House, Bexton Road, Knutsford, Cheshire, WA16 OBU.

Doreen M. Miller   Occupational Medicine Consultant, Registrar, Faculty of Occupational Medicine, Royal College of Physicians, 6 St Andrews Place, Regents Park, London, NW1 4LB. (Formerly Chief Medical Officer, Marks & Spencer plc.)

David A. Moore   Director of Group Medical Services, Occupational Health & Safety Services, Scottish & Newcastle plc, 149 Fountainbridge, Edinburgh, EH3 9RL.

Shirley Reynolds   Research Clinical Psychologist, MRC/ ESRC Social and Applied Psychology Unit, Department of Psychology, University of Sheffield, Sheffield, S10 2TN.

Eric L. Teasdale   Chief Medical Officer and Manager, International SHE Dept., Zeneca Pharmaceuticals, Alderley House, Alderley Edge, Macclesfield, Cheshire, SK10 4TF.

Robert Willcox   Group Medical Officer, Cable and Wireless plc, New Mercury House, 26 Red Lion Square, London, WC1R 4UQ.

Foreword

JOHN BOWIS, MP
Parliamentary Under Secretary of State for Health

There is a considerable cost to people, in both human and financial terms, in working in an unhealthy stressful environment. It is therefore in businesses own interests to create healthy workplaces.

The Government s health strategy, set out *The Health of the Nation* white paper, recognised that the workplace is a key setting for improving health. A task force has examined what health promotion is being carried out in the workplace and made a number of recommendations about how it can be developed. A steering group will oversee the implementation of these recommendations, which are particularly concerned with building on what has already been achieved and finding ways of developing effective collaborative working between the key interests of health and safety, occupational health and health promotion in the private and public sectors at national and local levels.

Among the specific topics covered in this book is company alcohol policy. The Health of the Nation white paper also outlines the Government's intention to promote workplace alcohol policies.

Although socially acceptable and widely enjoyed, alcohol, if misused, can have serious physical and social consequences in many areas of life including the workplace. The cost to the economy of misuse of alcohol at work is estimated at £2 billion per year; these costs are based on premature mortality through alcohol-related illness, the cost of unemployment and long-term sickness absence.

We need to increase the understanding of employers and employees of the effects of alcohol on their performance at work and the consequent risks of physical harm involved when operating machinery, driving, etc., as well as the risks of taking important decisions when judgement is impaired.

All companies should have company alcohol policies, which address these issues and recognise the important contribution they can make to healthy work organisations.

It is also important that we focus on the mental health in the work force. It is estimated that 2 or 3 out of every 10 employees will experience a mental health problem at some stage of their career. Untreated mental health problems, particularly anxiety and depression, result in substantial occupational problems, such as sickness absence (91 million working days lost in 1991 alone), reduced productivity, higher staff turnover, and poor concentration and judgement, leading to bad decisions and accidents at work. These result in significant costs to industry, estimated by the CBI at around £5.3 billion annually. Clearly, then, the importance of developing strategies to combat mental ill-health in the workplace cannot be underestimated.

However, much work needs to be done. In 1991, a CBI survey of all its members, sponsored by the Department of Health, found that although 95% of respondents thought that the mental health of employees should be of concern to their employers, only 13% had a company policy or programme related to mental health. The Government, therefore, has adopted a strategy of collaboration with employers to increase their awareness of mental health at work and the value, both to employees and the business, of a proactive approach to the creation of a healthy workplace. A Mental Health at Work task group which draws together the CBI and other interested parties has also been established within the Department of Health to provide a forum for the planning of prevention strategies to be implemented in the workplace.

The Government launched its public information strategy on mental illness in March 1993. A resource pack is being produced as part of this strategy which people involved in mental health promotion can use to provide information to the public. *Mental Health at Work* was, in October 1993, the second book to be published under the public information strategy. The booklet is aimed at employers and employees and describes the components of a good workplace mental health policy and some of the actions that employers can take.

I hope this book will help employers and employees alike to recognise the benefits of healthy workplaces and encourage all concerned to work together to create healthy workplace organisations.

Series Preface

The purpose of this series of books is to highlight the relationship between work, well-being and stress. It is intended that this series will explore topics such as managing organizational stress, worksite health programmes, burnout among human service professionals, employee assistance programmes, the nature and control of violence in the workplace and many other topics. We anticipate that this series will appeal to both the academic community and practitioners in the fields of occupational health, human resource management and industrial/occupational/organizational psychology.

We open the series with a book which attempts to provide "good practice" examples of what public and private sectors companies can do in *Creating Healthy Work Organizations*. This edited volume is comprised of contributions from several leading occupational health physicians from some world-leading companies. They illustrate good practice in health promotion in policies and programmes in workplace alcohol abuse, in a corporate wellness programme, in a corporate mental-health policy, in work redesign to improve worker control, in physical and mental health screening, and in managing stress at work. It is hoped that this volume will launch a series of books that will help to identify and improve the climate and health of work organizations.

CLC
January 1994

1
The Costs of Healthy Work Organizations

CARY L. COOPER
Manchester School of Management, UMIST

Work, is, by its very nature, about violence—to the spirit as well as to the body. It is about ulcers as well as accidents, about shouting matches as well as fistfights, about nervous breakdowns as well as kicking the dog around. It is, above all (or beneath all), about daily humiliations. To survive the day is triumph enough for the walking wounded among the great many of us.

(Studs Terkel, *Working*)

Unhealthy work organizations, as the above quotation illustrates, can create enormous human and financial costs. The occupational mental and physical ill health bill to business and industry in monetary terms has become increasingly well documented. For example, US industry loses approximately 550 million working days each year due to absenteeism. In terms of job and organizational generated problems, it has been estimated that 54% of these absences are in some way stress-related (Elkin & Rosch, 1990), that is, created by an unhealthy work environment. Recent figures released by the Confederation of British Industry (Sigman, 1992) calculate that in the UK, 360 million working days are lost annually through sickness, at a cost to organizations of £8 billion. Again, it has

Creating Healthy Work Organizations. Edited by C. L. Cooper and S. Williams.
© 1994 John Wiley & Sons Ltd

been estimated by the UK Health and Safety Executive that at least half of these lost days are related to workplace stress. In addition to the direct costs of sickness absence, labour turnover and the like, there are also indirect costs. The most obvious is what is being termed 'presenteeism', that is, the huge costs to public and private sector organizations of people turning up to work, who are so distressed by their jobs or some aspect of the organizational climate that they contribute little, if anything, to their work. The costs come in the form of lack of added value to the product or service rendered, or indeed, even a decrement to performance, in the sense that additional labour or materials are required to rectify the poor quality product or service. This is the great hidden cost of stress at work, that is, of not adequately creating the work environments that lead to enhanced well-being and productivity.

Physical and mental illnesses are also increasing in society at large, as well as in industry. For example, the United Kingdom continues to be near the top of the league table for mortality due to heart disease, for both men and women. Increasingly, evidence is emerging that the occupational and psycho-social factors such as stress at work are implicated in heart disease. Russek and Zohman (1958) compared young coronary patients between 25 and 40 years of age with healthy controls, and found that 91% of the coronary patients reported prolonged stress related to work responsibilities, compared to only 20% of the control patients. In addition, 25% were previously coping with two jobs, an additional 46% had been working 60 hours or more per week, and 20% reported frustration, discontent, insecurity or inadequacies associated with their job. More recently, Alfredsson, Karasek, Theorell, Schwartz and Pieper (1982) demonstrated in a case-controlled study that increased risk of heart attacks was associated with work and occupations characterized by hectic work and low control over the degree of variety and work pace. Last year, the British Heart Foundation published data on the costs of heart disease alone to the private and public sector: (i) 21% of all male absence from work is caused by heart and circulatory disease, (ii) 45% of all premature deaths of working people between 35 and 64 are caused by heart disease, and finally (iii) for a company of 10 000 employees the following costs will be incurred in any one year:

(a) the company will lose £2.1 million in lost productive value for men and £340 000 for women due to heart disease, (b) they will also lose 35 men and 7 women due to coronary death and (c) they will lose nearly 59 000 working days for men and 14 200 for women due to problems associated with coronary heart disease. This is a staggering bill for industry, the economy and the National Health Service, and one that can to some extent be avoided. And it must be remembered that heart disease is only one of the physical manifestations of an unhealthy organization, research shows that there are many more possible diseases and negative healthy outcomes (e.g. gastro-intestinal disorders, immune system failures, neuro-logical problems, etc.) (Cooper & Watson, 1991; Cooper & Payne, 1991).

As well as physical complaints and illnesses due to unhealthy work environments, days lost each year due to psychological disorders or reduced mental health such as nervous debility, tension headaches and mental breakdowns continue to show an increase (Cartwright & Cooper, 1994). Healthcare costs for mental illness are reported to exceed $36 billion each year in the US, with the costs to industry identified by the National Institute of Occupational Safety and Health as being $22 billion in terms of decreased productivity and lost employment. Furthermore, a link between mental health and accident involvement has consistently been reported. Carter and Corlett (1981) found that a review of the literature in the field suggested that 'the mental state of the operator, whether he is fatigued or over-aroused, alert or distracted has been the most frequently suggested reason for accident-causation during shiftwork'. In the UK, the number of days lost to mental and stress-related causes has mounted, as work environments have become more stressful and less 'people friendly' (Cooper & Payne, 1988). In addition to these obvious direct costs, we can now add the potential costs of employee litigation or workers' compensation claims.

For many years now, employees in the US have been litigating against their employers not only for poor environ-mental and physical contributions at work, but also for job-related stress or what they term 'cumulative trauma' in the workplace (Cooper, Cooper & Eaker, 1988). For example, in

California the stress-related compensation claims for psychiatric injury now total over 3000 a year, since the California Supreme Court upheld its first stress disability case in the early 1970s. The California Labor Code now states specifically that workers' compensation is allowable for disability or illness caused by 'repetitive mentally or physically traumatic activities extending over a period of time, the combined effect of which causes any disability or need for medical treatment'. The first 'cumulative trauma' or stress at work cases are currently being deliberated by the High Court in the UK, and many more cases are in the lower courts. The UK courts are likely, therefore, to accept 'stress caused by the job and/or the work organization' as an industrial injury in the near future.

In addition to these negative motivations for employers to create healthy work cultures, in the last few years there has been an explosion of health promotion or 'wellness' programmes in US and UK industry. Such activities as exercise, stress management training, smoking cessation and counselling are being encouraged by virtually every medium available—radio, TV, magazines, books—and are taking place not only in the home, schools, etc., but also in the workplace. Indeed, it is the primary purpose of this volume to provide 'best practice' examples of such programmes in UK industry, by highlighting corporate interventions to create healthy work organizations.

The next chapter in the book will outline a framework for understanding the different kinds of workplace interventions in healthy organizations. From then on we will highlight, in each subsequent chapter, attempts to create healthy work cultures, by drawing on the interventions of practitioners in the field, in major international organizations, to achieve employee and corporate health. Each of these case studies or prescriptive suggestions can inadvertently move us toward more 'liveable work cultures'. If we can only keep the words of Kornhauser (1965) in mind, we should be on the right track:

Mental health is not so much a freedom from specific frustrations as it is an overall balanced relationship to the world, which permits a person to maintain a realistic, positive belief in himself and his purposeful activities. Insofar as his entire job and life situation facilitate and support such feelings of adequacy, inner security, and meaningfulness of his existence, it can be presumed that his mental health will tend to be good. What is important in a negative way is not any single characteristic of his situation but everything that deprives the person of purpose and zest, that leaves him with negative feelings about himself, with anxieties, tensions, a sense of lostness, emptiness, and futility.

REFERENCES

Alfredsson, L., Karasek, R. A., Theorell, T. G. T., Schwartz, J. & Pieper, C. (1982). Job, psychosocial factors and coronary heart disease. In *Psychological problems before and after myocardial infarction, Advanced Cardiology*, Vol. 29 (ed. H. Denolin). Basle: Karger.

Carter, F. A. & Corlett, E. N. (1981). Shiftwork and accidents. *Report to the European Foundation for the Improvement of Living and Working Conditions*, Dublin, Ireland, 1982.

Cartwright , S. & Cooper, C. L. (1994). *No Hassle: Taking the Stress Out of Work*. London: Century Books.

Cooper, C. L., Cooper, R. D. & Eaker, L. (1988). *Living with Stress*. London: Penguin Books.

Cooper, C. L. & Payne, R. (1988). *Causes, Coping and Consequences of Stress at Work*. Chichester and New York: Wiley.

Cooper, C. L. & Payne, R. (1991). *Personality and Stress: Individual Differences in the Stress Process*. Chichester and New York: Wiley.

Cooper, C. L. & Watson, M. (1991). *Cancer and Stress: Psychological, Biological and Coping Studies*. Chichester and New York: Wiley.

Elkin, A. J. & Rosch, P. J. (1990). Promoting mental health at the workplace. *Occupational Medicine: State of the Art Review*, **5** (4), 734–754.

Kornhauser, A. (1965). *Mental Health of the Industrial Worker*. New York: Wiley.

Russek H. I. & Zohman, B. L. (1958). Relative significance of heredity, diet and occupational stress in C.H.D. of young adults. *American Journal of Medical Sciences*, **235**, 266–275.

Sigman, A. (1992). The state of corporate health care. *Personnel Management*, February 1992, 24–31.

2
Ways of Creating Healthy Work Organizations

STEPHEN WILLIAMS
Resource Assessment and Development, Harrogate

INTRODUCTION

Positive change starts with the recognition of the need to change and a clear vision of the outcome of the change process. Healthy organizations are not created by accident. We need to manage the health of our employees as carefully as we manage our organization and the most effective way of improving the well-being of our staff is through the implementation of a planned programme of health initiatives.

Health at work covers a wide range of issues from a basic concern with health and safety to the more contentious areas of counselling and 'lifestyle' management. This chapter provides a framework for the discussion of the various aspects of organizational health, and categorizes these elements into a four-level structure, the 'organizational health grid'. This structure is based on the World Health Organization (WHO) and

Creating Healthy Work Organizations. Edited by C. L. Cooper and S. Williams.
© 1994 John Wiley & Sons Ltd

International Labour Organization (ILO) definition of the aims of occupational health as:

> the promotion and maintenance of the highest degree of physical, mental and social well-being of workers in all occupations by prevention of departures from health, and controlling risks.

The working environment has a significant impact on all aspects of employee health and, in order to focus attention on this issue, environmental factors are included with the physical, mental and social health dimensions mentioned in the WHO definition. The four elements of organizational health are therefore:

● Environmental Factors
● Physical Health
● Mental (Psychological) Health
● Social Health

Each of these elements has a variety of definitions, and attempts to reach a consensus on the definition of terms, such as social health, have met with failure (Russell, 1973). This chapter is concerned with the practical use of the four dimensions of organizational health as an aid to creating healthy organizations. In this context, precise definitions of the terms are not essential provided the aspects of health covered by each of the four elements are understood. The following brief descriptions of each of the four elements should be sufficient to enable them to be used as a framework for categorizing health initiatives.

Environmental factors concern all aspects of the work environment and include factors such as noise levels, hazardous substances, temperature, the physical work area, machine guards, and workplace design. Physical health includes fitness, diet, disease, injury, medication and lifting and handling. Mental health deals with factors such as self-esteem, stress, depression, anxiety, and behavioural style. Social health involves companionship, life events such as redundancy or marital break-up, social support, relationships at work, and outside interests.

This list is not exhaustive and the border between the categories is not clearly delineated. Organizations need to take a holistic approach to managing the health of their employees and be aware of the interaction between the various elements. Depression, for example, may be caused by a combination of environmental, physical and social factors. A structured approach to the analysis of organizational health must, therefore, take into account the interactions among the four categories and the extent to which they overlap.

THE ORGANIZATIONAL HEALTH GRID

Figure 2.1 shows how the four elements of organizational health can be incorporated into a formal structure. It clarifies the interaction between the elements and illustrates a progression from the basic environmental factors to the social factors. The grid structure represents a series of steps from environmental concerns to social issues, and the grid suggests a hierarchy of organizational health similar to Maslow's hierarchy of needs (Maslow, 1943). In the health grid, the environmental and physical elements correspond with Maslow's description of an individual's basic physiological and safety and security needs. It seems reasonable to assume that employees need a safe working environment, and will not be concerned with other aspects of health promotion until this basic need is satisfied. This means that organizations must ensure that the basic health and safety needs of employees are met before more sophisticated interventions can be considered.

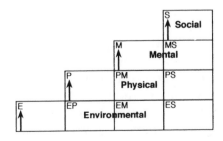

Figure 2.1   *The organizational health grid*

For example, there is little point in introducing an Employee Assistance Programme to help with psychological and social problems if the working environment is toxic or hazardous. Although progress through the four levels need not be sequential, it seems sensible to ensure that the environmental factors, the foundation stones of good health, are correct before considering other health initiatives.

The health grid provides a systematic framework for identifying ways of creating healthy organizations by drawing attention to each of the ten zones created by the overlap of the four elements. For example, the environmental and social factors intersect at the bottom right of the grid in the zone labelled ES. This zone represents the Environmental–Social (ES) issues, and includes topics such as the provision of informal meeting areas, the layout of open plan offices, the social use of internal telephone and network systems and so on. Each of the six combination zones EP, EM, ES, PM, PS, and MS can act as a prompt for developing specific health initiatives. An analysis of the Environment–Physical (EP) zone may stimulate discussion of the ergonomic issues or suggest the building of a fitness centre or a review of the smoking policy. Initiatives in the Physical–Social (PS) zone might include activities such as Outward Bound courses that combine physical exercise with social interaction. Similar examples can be given for each of the zones, and it is possible to use the grid to produce a list of initiatives covering every aspect of organizational health. This list can be prioritized and used to develop a planned organizational health improvement programme.

IMPLEMENTING AND MONITORING CHANGE

Once the organization has decided what it wants to achieve in developing the health of its employees, it needs to be able to implement the plan and monitor progress. The old adage, 'if you can't measure it, you can't manage it' is a useful reminder of the need to show the extent to which the organization is able to realize its objectives. For example, an organization may review its current health and safety programmes and decide it needs to place more emphasis on mental health issues. Figure 2.2

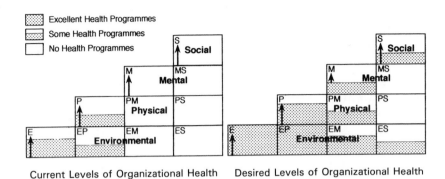

Current Levels of Organizational Health   Desired Levels of Organizational Health

Figure 2.2   *Planned change in organizational health*

uses the health grid to show the current and desired levels of organizational health on each of the four dimensions. The health grid helps to make the stages involved in moving from the 'current' to the 'desired' state explicit, and focuses attention on the relevant issues.

The organization needs to know if the health initiatives are producing the desired effect. Simple measures, such as sickness absence, provide an overall indication of the health of the workforce, but may not reflect the true nature and extent of employee well-being. Other measures such as staff turnover, accidents at work, and productivity are influenced by a multiplicity of factors, not all of which are work-related. It is useful to know whether specific interventions produce measurable improvements in employee health and the health grid can be used to suggest appropriate measures. For example, an attitude survey may provide information about improvements in social health; a reduction in accident rates may demonstrate the effectiveness of environmental improvements.

The Policy Statement

Creating a healthy organization is not a passive process in which employee health is a by-product of complying with legislation. It should be part of the strategic development of the organization and the responsibility of the Chief Executive and the Board. However, few organizations in the United Kingdom appear to give this level of attention to employee health. A 1985 survey by the Employment Medical Advisory Service showed that over 75% of the firms surveyed had no occupational health service other than the statutory requirement of first aid. This situation needs to change and the first step in creating a healthy organization is to make the promotion of the health of the workforce a declared objective with a policy statement showing how this is to be achieved. The 1974 Health and Safety at Work Act requires every employer with more than 5 employees to produce a written statement on their general policy on health and safety at work. The statement should set out the arrangements for carrying out the policy and be revised wherever appropriate. All employees must be made aware of the contents of the policy statement and any subsequent revisions. The Health and Safety at Work Act lays down the minimum requirement for a health policy, and healthy organizations will ensure that their policy statement goes beyond the minimum to emphasize the promotion of good health and provide a clear mandate for action.

Strategies for Change

The change process should begin with a clear understanding of the objectives of the change programme. Organizations should decide what they mean by a healthy workplace, assess their performance on each of the four dimensions of health, and prioritize their interventions. The health grid provides one possible framework for action and organizations may use a variety of techniques for developing a planned improvement programme. The overall objective of the change programme can be summarized by the need to create an organization that:

> Actively manages the promotion and maintenance of the highest levels of physical mental and social well-being of its employees.

The key phrase in this description of a healthy organization is *'actively manages'*. Traditionally occupational health has emphasized the remedial aspects of healthcare, however, since the early 1980s there has been a growing awareness of the need for much broader preventive activity. More recently the popular interest in 'healthy living' has been supported by the development of general workplace health promotion programmes. Occupational health has evolved from a concern with work-related hazards to the development of the all round well-being of the individual. The changing role of occupational health and the wide variety of possible health initiatives makes it important to keep sight of the key issues. The essentials of good employee health care should not be overlooked.

Key Issues

The key issues facing organizations in developing employee health were reported in a recent survey of major UK employers' associations and trades unions (Smith & Jacobson, 1988). The survey aimed to provide a general impression of the way occupational health was interpreted in practice by major employers and trade unions, and Table 2.1 shows the ranking of the key issues for health in the workplace.

The list shows that the traditional environmental concerns of noise, safety and dust have the highest priority and reinforces the importance of environmental factors in organizational health. Physical health issues are also a priority, as is stress.

Table 2.1

Highest priority	No priority
Noise	Contraception
Safety	Sexually transmitted disease
Dusts	Personal development
Muscular/chemical hazards	
Alcohol	
Smoking	
Stress	
Nutrition	

Source: Webb, T., Schilling, R., Jacobson, B. & Babb, P. (1988). Health at work?: A report on health promotion in the workplace. HEA Research Report 22. London: Health Education Authority. Reproduced by permission.

The list supports the hierarchy of organizational health issues illustrated by the health grid, and indicates the work that needs to be done to improve the basic building blocks of employee health before social issues such as personal development become important.

Organizations are running programmes to improve health at work in all of these areas, and the following chapters give examples of a broad range of physical, mental and social initiatives. The remainder of this chapter describes a number of environmental initiatives and gives a brief overview of the physical, mental and social health issues.

ENVIRONMENTAL INITIATIVES

Working conditions have improved enormously over the past 50 years. The days when workers were exposed to toxic chemicals, dangerous machines, and exploitative working practices are, hopefully, behind us. As a result of legislation and more enlightened management, the vast majority of employees in the Western economies can expect, at the very least, a basic standard of safety, comfort and cleanliness at their place of work. However, the working environment has a tendency to deteriorate and employees can slip into bad practices. What was once a healthy workplace can, gradually and imperceptibly, become potentially damaging. Most people just get on with their jobs. They put up with filing cabinets with sticking drawers, wires that trail across the floor, flickering fluorescent tubes, fluctuations in heating, constant background noise, uncomfortable seating and so on. They tolerate these aspects of working in a modern office or factory or shop because 'it's part of the job'. Employees accept, unless things are obviously wrong, what they are given and, as days go on, cease to notice that there is a problem. The faulty fluorescent tube and badly adjusted VDU start to cause headaches but the environmental issues, the source of the problem, are never addressed. Organizations concerned with creating and maintaining a healthy working environment should, in addition to any statutory requirements, regularly audit the extent to which they comply with the legislation and adhere to good working practice.

One of the most important environmental factors in organizational health is the control of hazardous substances. Although this factor is most commonly associated with industrial processes, every employee can be at risk if the right precautions are not taken. The Control of Substances Hazardous to Health (COSHH) regulations lay down the essential requirements for managing risk and employers are required to:

- Assess the risk to health arising from the work done and decide what precautions are needed
- Introduce appropriate measures to prevent or control the risk
- Ensure that control measures are used and that equipment is properly maintained and procedures observed
- Where necessary, monitor the exposure of the workers and carry out an appropriate form of surveillance of their health
- Inform, instruct and train employees about the risks and the precautions to be taken

Environmental initiatives should be supported by workplace education. According to Health and Safety Executive (HSE) figures, a quarter of all fatal accidents at work involve failures in systems of work. The 1974 Health and Safety at Work Act requires all employers 'to provide systems of work that are, so far as reasonably practicable, safe and without risks to health'. This means that employees working in areas where hazards cannot be eliminated need to observe safe working practices. They need to understand the dangers associated with incorrect handling, exposure to noise and fumes, VDU eyestrain, slippery floors and countless other workplace hazards. Prevention is always better than cure and prevention begins with knowing the risks and how to avoid them.

Most production managers, for example, are familiar with the problem of enforcing the use of safety glasses or ear protectors. New employees, as part of their induction training, will be made aware of the need for safety equipment but, within a few days of being on the factory floor and observing more experienced workers flaunting the rules, they will ignore what they have been told. Managers need to be vigilant and constantly remind employees of the need to protect themselves from the dangers of the workplace.

The wearing of safety glasses and hard hats is easy to monitor but compliance becomes more difficult to enforce when good practice is hard to observe. It isn't always easy for supervisors to spot when VDU operators don't take breaks or when supermarket checkout operators twist their bodies as they lift heavy items across the bar code scanner. It is the responsibility of the employer to make the individual aware of the risks and to encourage them to follow the health and safety guidelines.

The majority of organizations, as well as improving health and safety education, can do a great deal to improve the way in which they draw attention to workplace risk. The workplace, whether it is the factory floor, a shop, office or building site, can be used to reinforce the messages presented in health education programmes. Signs, warning lights, floor markings, colour codes, posters and promotional displays can all act as reminders to promote good practice. The principles of the visual factory (Greif, 1991) can be used throughout the workplace to promote good health as well as increased productivity.

In creating healthy organizations employers should ensure that the way in which people do their jobs is in keeping with the best environmental and ergonomic principles, and be sensitive to the impact of the work environment on the psychological and social as well as physical health of their employees.

PHYSICAL HEALTH INITIATIVES

The range of physical health initiatives has expanded dramatically in recent years as occupational health specialists have become increasingly aware of the close relationship between an individual's lifestyle and their health. Lifestyle is now seen as the most significant factor in good health, and this has prompted organizations to place more emphasis on health screening and education programmes.

Research has shown that helping employees to understand more about the risks they are exposed to, and the actions they can take to reduce those risks, is a powerful tool for creating a healthy workforce. Although physical health screening is the most frequently used method of raising awareness of individual risk factors, employees need to be aware of the risks involved in every aspect of working life including mechanical handling procedures, the dangers of alcohol and drug abuse, and stress at work.

In the past, health screening at work tended to be restricted to senior executives who enjoyed the benefit of an annual medical. A growing number of organizations are now extending the scope of health screening with the major health care providers offering comprehensive programmes for all employees. Table 2.2 shows the range of screening services provided by BMI Healthcare, one of the leading companies in this field.

The screening services provide employees with detailed information about their health and identify the factors that put their health at risk. Organizations have a responsibility to help their staff to act on that information by providing a health education service that shows them how to reduce the risks

Table 2.2 *Screening services provided by BMI Healthcare*

Cardiovascular Risk Assessment	This includes a computer-based appraisal of heart disease and smoke risks
Menopause Assessment	A programme including examination by a physician and discussion of symptom treatment options
Well Woman	This includes examination by a physician for general health assessment and detection of early signs of female-specific cancers
Well Man	This programme includes a physician's examination for general health and heart disease risk assessment and early detection of signs of male-specific cancers
Heart Screen	A full assessment including physical examination and resting and exercising electrocardiograms of coronary artery condition
Health Screen	A comprehensive check for either sex for the most important health risk causes in both sexes, including heart disease and cancers

and improve their health. These education programmes need to address every aspect of health raised by the screening process, and will inevitably be broad-based and include mental and social as well as physical health initiatives. The most frequently used initiatives include education programmes on:

- Heart disease
- Cholesterol
- Blood pressure
- Exercise
- Smoking
- Obesity
- Alcohol
- Stress
- Cancer
- Nutrition
- AIDS

The introduction of a wide range of screening services raises the question of who is responsible for workplace health, the employer or the employee? Does it matter if an employee is overweight, has high levels of cholesterol and an excess of alcohol in his blood? As long as he or she can continue to do their job is their physical, mental and social health relevant? Do employers have a right to know about the problems and, if they do, do they have a responsibility to help? These questions need to be answered before an organization introduces screening services or other health programmes. The employee needs to know how the information from the screening programme will be used and the range of follow-up services the organization can provide. Confidentiality is an important issue and employers should be aware that some people will worry about the results of their screening being misused. For example, the recession has made many people feel insecure and employees have been known to voice their concern that health screening is linked to selection for redundancy. These fears need to be allayed and all eligible employees should be encouraged to go through the screening process.

MENTAL HEALTH INITIATIVES

Mental health is a function of an individual's physical and social well-being. It is not a separate entity. Work has a significant influence on mental health and Table 2.3 shows some of the main factors. Despite the wide range of factors listed in the table, mental health is an issue which a great many organizations are still reluctant to discuss or recognize. It is an employer's duty to provide a safe environment for their employees and there is a general acceptance of the need to promote good physical health. The promotion of mental health at work is more controversial. The 1992 joint Department of Health and CBI Conference on promoting mental health at work set out the agenda for raising the awareness of mental health at the workplace and urged employers to change their attitudes to mental illness. Unfortunately, the majority of

Table 2.3 *Main work factors influencing mental health*

Organizational Factors	Working conditions
	Perceived hazards
	Ergonomics
	Organizational structure and climate
	Level of involvement
	Change and innovation
	Poor management
Individual Factors	Injury or illness
	Job insecurity
	Over- or underpromotion
	Too much or too little work
	Change in the nature of work
	Role conflict or ambiguity
	Irregular or long hours
	Lack of influence
	Lack of stimulation
Social Factors	Family illness or bereavement
	Marital or family problems
	Conflict between home and work
	Actual or potential violence
	Relocation
	Financial difficulties

organizations still do not discuss the mental health of their employees. This is in spite of the fact that at least 6 million people in the UK suffer from some sort of mental illness in the course of a year (Jenkins & Coney, 1992).

The starting point for a programme to improve mental health at work must be to acknowledge that it is a legitimate concern of the organization and a key element of the health promotion strategy. Organizations need to be open about their role in improving the mental health of their employees and take steps to help individuals to recognize the risk factors and take preventive action. See Chapter 6, by Ann Fingret, which provides an excellent blueprint for introducing a mental health plan.

SOCIAL INITIATIVES

We live in a world of constant change and the rate of change is accelerating. We inflict change on our employees and expect them to adapt to the new situation without complaint. Most employees understand that change is inevitable but they have difficulty in adjusting to seemingly irrelevant changes in structure or working methods. In many cases, managers fail to consider the impact of change on their staff. They look at the business needs or the impact on customers and overlook the effect on their employees. Healthy organizations consider the impact of change on their staff and take steps to prevent avoidable disruption.

The way an organization communicates with its employees is a major factor in the promotion of mental and social health. Good communications go hand in hand with good management and are an essential feature of the healthy organization. There are a wide range of techniques for improving communications and managers need to continually develop their communication systems at both an individual and an organizational level. Open, honest communication is the basis of trust between management and employees. It leads to mutual respect and helps the employee to feel valued.

Another important aspect of social health is the balance between work and home. Many people find it difficult to avoid a conflict between work and home and a large number of managers still equate effectiveness with long hours. There is a strongly held belief in British industry that the only way to be successful is to work longer than your colleagues. Britain has one of the longest working weeks in Europe and an increasing number of people feel that the balance between home and work is out of alignment. Some people enjoy their work so much that they want to be there as much as possible. For example, young people living in small flats or shared accommodation or even at home with parents, may find being at work more sociable and more enjoyable than being at home. The problem comes for those people who want to spend more time at home but feel forced to work long hours. Organizations need to be aware of the demands that they make on their employees and help them to achieve a balance between home and work.

One of the most interesting developments in the promotion of social health is the growth of flexible working arrangements. Flexible working includes job sharing, part-time work, working from home, flexible hours, and location-independent working. New technologies enable employers to reduce the cost of office accommodation and make it easy for a growing number of employees to achieve a better balance between home and work. Although full flexible working may not be appropriate for everyone, organizations should look for ways of introducing some element of flexibility into their work patterns. Even a limited degree of flexibility, such as being able to take a shorter lunch break and leave earlier, may give an extra few hours a week for a mother to spend with her children or help a commuter to get back in time for an evening class.

A recent development in the promotion of social health has been the growth of employee assistance programmes (EAPs). EAPs provide a confidential advisory service to employees and cover a wide range of issues including help with financial, marital and domestic problems as well as mental and physical health issues. The role of the EAPs is discussed in detail in Chapter 11.

Perhaps the ultimate objective of social health programmes is to make work 'fun' for all employees. If the organization is able to stimulate and reward the individual then employees can learn, grow and develop throughout their working career.

They will enjoy the challenge and respond positively to pressure. Work will add to their sense of well-being and a positive, happy, enthusiastic workplace will mean a healthy workforce.

In the end the development of health at work comes down to organizational values. How does the organization treat its employees? Are people really its most important asset? Organizations should respect their employees, encourage their achievements and treat them fairly. Healthy organizations are created through a planned programme of environmental, physical, psychological and social initiatives. These initiatives need to be recognized as the legitimate concern of the business and the cause of good health championed within the organization. Success in creating a healthy workforce is measured by the extent to which organizations actively promote the health of their staff. We spend almost one-third of our waking lives at work and we ought to benefit from it physically, mentally and socially as well as financially.

THE STRUCTURE OF THE BOOK

The following chapters are case studies in the development of healthy organizations They show how a variety of organizations have addressed the problem of improving the health of their employees, and are organized according to their emphasis on either physical, mental or social health. Chapter 3 describes the development of a corporate wellness programme in Nestlé UK and covers the four dimensions of health. The chapter provides a detailed case study of how Nestlé integrated a variety of occupational health initiatives into a comprehensive programme. The corporate wellness programme addresses the four dimensions of organizational health, and has been developed from the commitment to provide all employees with a safe and healthy working environment. The programme monitors workplace risks including noise, dust and other environmental issues and identifies physical and mental health issues through a variety of risk factor screening programmes including coronary risk and stress at work. It also describes some of the interventions, such as the fitness programme.

Chapter 4 deals with a combination of physical and mental health initiatives, and describes the way that Cable & Wireless plc has developed an effective primary health care programme capable of offering positive health screening to several thousand people a year. The chapter outlines the basic principles underlying employee health screening and covers a range of screening programmes including coronary risk assessment, stress profiles and the development of eye and fitness assessments. It also includes a summary of research undertaken by Cable & Wireless into the effectiveness of screening as an intervention mechanism. Chapter 5 deals with a specific aspect of organizational health, a workplace alcohol abuse programme. The chapter describes the Scottish and Newcastle Breweries experience of designing and implementing a workplace alcohol programme.

The next four chapters explore a variety of approaches to improving mental health at work. Chapter 6 sets the scene by outlining a four-stage programme for the development of a mental health plan. The chapter provides an effective blueprint for organizations wishing to develop and implement their own programmes to improve mental health at work. The starting point for a mental health plan is the assessment of the organization structure and culture, and Chapter 7 focuses on one specific assessment mechanism. This latter chapter describes BNR Europe's experiences of identifying the nature and extent of stress at work by carrying out a stress audit. The chapter describes the process of running the audit and the actions that BNR took to improve the stress profiles of their employees. Chapter 8 also deals with the issue of stress at work, and describes how ICI/Zeneca Pharmaceuticals developed a series of stress management workshops. The chapter summarizes Zeneca's experience of running and evaluating the workshops over the past seven years, and shows the success of the intervention programme in improving the mental health of the participants. Chapter 9 describes a number of initiatives taken by North Derbyshire Health Authority to improve the physical and psychological well-being of their healthcare staff. The chapter discusses a variety of approaches to improving mental health, including both personal and organizational interventions.

The next two chapters explore social health initiatives. Chapter 10 describes the way in which Marks & Spencer plc has dealt with some of the issues of stress at work by dealing with the fundamental issues of control and influence within their organization. The chapter describes the implementation of a continuous improvement programme designed to give shop-based employees the opportunity to influence their workplace environment. It describes how the health services within Marks & Spencer identified a range of physical, psychological and social health issues that were primarily caused by a lack of influence, and addressed these issues at source by developing a continuous improvement programme. Chapter 11 also deals with social health, and describes the role of Employee Assistance Programmes in creating healthy work organizations. It outlines the development of Employee Assistance Programmes and the range of services offered by the assistance programme provider.

The final chapter of this book provides a simple checklist for identifying the extent to which an organization is actively managing the health of its employees, and proposes an action plan for creating healthier work organizations.

REFERENCES

Greif, M. (1991). *The Visual Factory, Building Participation through Shared Information*. Cambridge: Productivity Press.

Jenkins, R. & Coney, N. (1992). *Prevention of Mental Ill Health at Work*. London: HMSO.

Maslow, A. H. (1943). A theory of human motivation, *Psychological Review*, 370–396.

Russell, R. D. (1973). Social health: An attempt to clarify this dimension of well-being. *International Journal of Health Education*, **16**/2, 74–84.

Smith, A. & Jacobson, K. (1988). *The Nation's Health—A Strategy for the 1990s*. London: King's Fund.

3
Development of a Corporate Wellness Programme: Nestlé UK Ltd

DAVID C. BATMAN
Group Chief Medical Officer, Nestlé UK Ltd, York

INTRODUCTION

Health screening and surveillance procedures are well practised throughout medicine as a tool to identify and monitor individuals with particular susceptibilities or risks and have been developed within Occupational Health Departments in relation to pre-employment and pre-placement examinations, return to work assessments, and surveillance of 'at-risk' groups such as food handlers and drivers. When used appropriately they provide an invaluable mechanism for managing work- and health-related issues which are of value to both the organisation and the employee.

However, over recent years there has been an increase in the 'executive medical' approach to health screening and other lifestyle-related examinations, largely developed around the 'cholesterol scare', but based on no sound rationale for introduction, management, quality control or follow-up.

Creating Healthy Work Organizations. Edited by C. L. Cooper and S. Williams.
© 1994 John Wiley & Sons Ltd

In 1988, the Rowntree Mackintosh confectionery business, later to become the Nestlé Rowntree Division of Nestlé UK Ltd, undertook a review of its Occupational Health Services and introduced a range of services, including a voluntary health screening programme, all of which were integrated to provide both the business and employees with an increased range of health programmes, services and facilities, upgrade the Occupational Health Departments and provide the occupational health staff with increased skills and awareness. These were to be additional to an already well-established health and safety programme.

This chapter highlights the introduction of the voluntary health screening programme by Rowntree Mackintosh during the period 1989 to 1992, employee results and the subsequent development of the programmes.

HISTORICAL PERSPECTIVE OF OCCUPATIONAL HEALTH WITHIN NESTLÉ ROWNTREE AND NESTLÉ UK LTD

In 1988, Rowntree plc was acquired by Nestlé SA and its UK confectionery business was integrated into a UK corporate business structure. In January 1992, Nestlé UK Ltd was formed and the confectionery business became the Nestlé Rowntree Division—one of four UK divisions covering 28 manufacturing sites and 14 transport depots.

Nestlé, within the UK, had developed similar occupational health services to Rowntree, and the beginning of 1992 saw the integration of all occupational health services into a Nestlé UK Ltd Occupational Health Service, working to the same standard across all 28 manufacturing sites and depots under the guidance of a Group Chief Medical Officer and Group Chief Nursing Officer.

The York site of Nestlé Rowntree was opened in 1891 by Rowntree & Co and has had an Occupational Health Department on site since 1904. Since its inception, this department has built a steady relationship with management, employees and unions, based on trust, confidentiality and the provision of services of relevance to both the business and employees. The Rowntree business always took pride in providing services for its employees in all aspects of life, and has not been slow in evaluating services in relation to the prevailing needs and implementing change where required. Prior to 1988, the Occupational Health Department provided a range of services to include pre-placement medicals, return to work assessments, on-site treatment services, supervision of food handlers, drivers and other 'at-risk' groups. Other services included chiropody, dentistry and the availability of a 28-bed convalescent home, called Dunollie, in nearby Scarborough—purchased in the mid 1940s when most NHS hospitals had attached homes to relieve hospital beds.

The services were designed to aid employees achieve maximum health with minimum delay in treatment and absence from work, recognising that employees were a most important business asset. These services were provided on the York site by a full-time Occupational Physician, a part-time medical officer, six full-time nursing staff (including one nurse whose sole responsibility was to visit employees at home when they were absent with long-term illnesses), two chiropodists and two dentists. A comparable range of services were provided on the other seven Rowntree sites by full- or part-time nurses and attending part-time medical officers who were general practitioners employed within the locality of the site.

Rationale for Introduction of Health Screening/Surveillance Programmes

In order for an Occupational Health Department to survive in the increasingly competitive nature of business, it must be able to integrate and work with all departments within a manufacturing site or other location. It can no longer exist in isolation as a 'reactive, first aid department', but must move towards a proactive/preventive position, developing services and programmes which will contribute towards business and employee objectives.

The Occupational Health Department must be able to fulfil three basic business functions:

1   Assist the business to meet its legal requirements—both HSE and increasingly EEC.
2   Assist the business to meet its own corporate objectives, which include health and safety, reduction in absence, commitment to employee well-being, increased productivity and profitability.
3   Provide services to employees to assist their awareness of health-related issues and subsequent management and risk reduction.

Nestlé UK recognises the contribution employees make towards the efficient running of a business and the problems caused by employee ill health to both the business, the employee and their family. There are clear benefits for all parties in preventing premature death or early retirement of employees, often at the height of their careers and experience.

An analysis of the predominant causes of morbidity and mortality affecting the employees of any company within the UK clearly demonstrates a range of illnesses which have lifestyle-related causes where a proactive approach adapted towards them could, and should, reduce their incidence.

The outstanding cause of death in the UK is coronary heart disease (CHD), causing 400 deaths per day in the UK and leading to the deaths of 1 in 3 males and 1 in 4 females between the ages of 55 and 64—a statistic which leads the world 'league

Table 3.1   *Causes of death in the UK*

Males	(%)	Females	(%)
Heart disease	19	Heart disease	7
Cerebro-vascular disease	4	Cerebro-vascular disease	5
Other circulatory disease	4	Other circulatory disease	4
Lung cancer	5	Breast cancer	12
Other cancers	16	Other cancers	23
Respiratory disease	6	Respiratory disease	5
Accidents	16	Accidents	8

table' for CHD deaths. Not a figure to be proud of! Clearly if there were to be an equivalent number of deaths in the UK due to a fully laden jumbo jet crashing at Heathrow every day, urgent measures would be adopted to correct the issue. The causes of CHD are largely lifestyle-related—but it was painfully obvious when talking to employees that they were unaware of the range of 'risk-factors', but were concentrating upon cholesterol levels only (Figure 3.1). If we were to encourage our employees to adopt a healthier lifestyle, it had to be a requirement that they were to be provided with a balanced approach to all their risk factors, in order to make a subjective assessment of their individual requirements. Without such an approach there is a danger of turning the 'well into the worried well'.

The development of any health screening programme had to encompass all of the above mentioned business and employee issues in order to be of value to all concerned. Where any business identified an issue or problem which could have a profound effect upon future production, it would undoubtedly produce a business plan to reduce or eliminate the risk—why then should not a similar approach be adopted to lifestyle-related health issues?

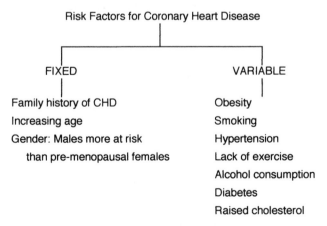

Figure 3.1 *Risk factors for coronary heart disease*

CRITERIA FOR INTRODUCTION

Having identified an employee 'health risk' for the future, the reduction of which could have a profound effect both upon the health of individual employees and on the business, a positive approach was adopted to producing a marketing strategy for risk management which included the creation and management of a corporate health screening programme (Figure 3.2).

Selection of the voluntary health screening and surveillance programme requirements was based upon the following criteria:

1 The programmes had to be available and acceptable to all regular employees.
2 Surveillance programmes to be available to monitor workplace risks, to include noise exposure, dusts, visual assessments of drivers and display screen users and management of food handlers.
3 Health screening programmes to be able to identify employee risk factors for lifestyle-related illnesses.
4 Any tests used must be acceptable to the workforce, sensitive, specific, repeatable, accurate, and cost-effective.

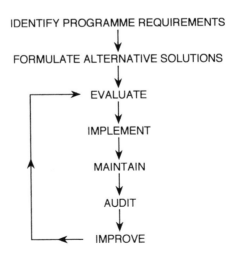

IDENTIFY PROGRAMME REQUIREMENTS

FORMULATE ALTERNATIVE SOLUTIONS

EVALUATE

IMPLEMENT

MAINTAIN

AUDIT

IMPROVE

Figure 3.2 *Marketing strategy for CHD risk reduction*

5 In relation to coronary heart disease the tests must be able to provide the employee with the ability to analyse all risk factors to gain a better perspective of risk.
6 The investigations should not turn the 'well' into the 'worried well'.
7 The same standard of programme to be available across all sites.
8 Screening equipment and delivery of information to be subject to quality control programmes.
9 All programmes should be subject to analysis, audit and review.

Once the criteria were agreed it was necessary to review from whom the services should be provided. An analysis of suitable vendors logically included:

1 Individual doctors
2 Private medical groups
3 Specialist screening companies
4 In-house Occupational Health Departments

In addition to meeting the programme requirements, it was deemed necessary that the vendor should also be required to have an understanding of business and any legal requirements, have competent staff conversant with screening techniques and delivery of results, have quality control programmes in use, be in a position to arrange follow-up of employees identified with health issues, be in a position to maintain confidentiality of results, and be cost-effective. After careful consideration it was decided that the most appropriate option was to develop the programmes within the existing company occupational health service.

OBJECTIVE AND AIMS OF THE VOLUNTARY HEALTH SCREENING PROGRAMME

Objective

To provide employees with a continuing programme of life-style evaluation, education and assistance to reduce the incidence of lifestyle-related ill health problems.

Aims

1 To provide a lifestyle awareness programme.
2 Employees to accept ownership of their health.
3 To encourage and assist employees to make lifestyle changes.
4 The programme to be available to all regular employees every three years.
5 OHS staff to be professionally trained in screening procedures.
6 The programme to be free, voluntary, confidential and in company time.
7 There to be a programme of quality control, audit and review.
8 To develop intervention strategies as appropriate.

Two programmes were designed—a general programme available to all regular employees every three years, administered by nursing staff, and the 'executive examination' which would be doctor-administered. The 'executive examination' to be doctor-controlled as, following market research within the group to be offered screening, it became obvious that they would not be prepared to discuss certain issues with staff of subordinate grades.

Voluntary Health Screening Programme Content

1 An in-house designed health screening questionnaire to be self-administered by the employee containing questions relating to family histories of coronary heart disease, hypertension, diabetes, cancer, cerebro-vascular disease, alcohol and nicotine consumption, and specific questions on symptoms they may or may not have been experiencing.
2 Examination of height, weight, blood pressure, pulse, and hygiene examination.
3 Urinalysis for albumin, blood and sugar.
4 Audiometry, lung function testing by vitalograph, visual assessment using a Keystone.

5 Cholesterol, haemoglobin, sugar and urea blood testing utilising desktop analysers.
6 The 'executive programme' had, in addition, a resting ECG, Occupational Stress Indicator analysis (OSI) and venous blood samples to include liver function tests and gamma GT.

The general programme is administered by Occupational Health Services nursing staff and the executive programme by Company Occupational Physicians.

Nursing staff undertook a three day training programme which included the rationale behind the programme, programme administration, equipment utilisation and quality control programmes, and results delivery to employees. A reference manual was produced available to all site OHS personnel trained to perform the programme. Standard equipment was purchased for all locations and appropriately installed, and individual sites developed 'screening rooms' as appropriate to location size and employee numbers.

PROGRAMME MANAGEMENT

Care and consideration were taken in the introduction of the programme to allay employee fears; the introduction of the programme could have been received with a certain degree of scepticism and worry, since at the time general practitioners were not offering health screening and an employee would only visit their medical practitioner when ill. It was alien to their health practice to visit a doctor when well! Articles were included in in-house newspapers, presentations were made to employees and union councils and an employee booklet was produced explaining the rationale behind the programme and programme contents.

A structured appointment system was developed to provide a managed approach to allow 13 000 employees access to the programme over a three year period. All employees in all age groups felt the need to attend at the earliest opportunity and it became obvious that the only rational way to manage the numbers of employees wishing to participate was to construct an age/sex register at each location to include all eligible employees. The register was designed initially to call all employees within the age group 35 to 45 alphabetically and then in 10-year age bands which would include employees in the 5-year age bands above and below the previous group. This would mean that by the end of the three-year recall period employees aged 16 and 65 would be being reviewed. While recognising that no system would suit all employees, this approach appeared to be acceptable to all parties.

Group 1   Ages 35 to 45, followed by,
Group 2   Ages 30 to 34 + 46 to 50, followed by,
Group 3   Ages 25 to 29 + 51 to 55, followed by,
Group 4   Ages 20 to 24 + 56 to 60, followed by,
Group 5   Ages 16 to 19 + 60 + .

Each employee eligible for the general programme is sent an appointment date (prior consultation being undertaken with line managers, to allow 60 mins off the production line), an explanatory booklet expanding on what is available, plus a health questionnaire to complete.

On arrival for their appointment, the supervising nurse will analyse the questionnaire with the employee and expand information where required. This has the advantage of allowing the employee to become more settled with the nurse and to ask any initial questions. During the ensuing 45 minutes the employee's height, weight, blood pressure and resting pulse are measured and urine tested for blood, protein and sugar.

Lung capacity is measured using a computerised vitalograph, hearing is evaluated using computerised audiometry within a sound proof booth, and vision is assessed using a keystone machine. Blood estimations of haemoglobin and cholesterol are measured using a finger tip capillary sample analysed using a reflotron desk top analyser.

On completion of the programme, the nurse and employee discuss the results of all the tests undertaken and analyse the totality of CHD risk factors, to allow the employee to take a balanced view of all parameters and avoid becoming preoccupied with individual factors.

The 'executive programme' is administered via a central register and each employee is given an initial 10-minute appointment at which a venous sample is taken and dispatched to an outside laboratory for analysis. At the same time they are provided with a copy of the Occupational Stress Indicator (OSI) (Cooper, Sloan & Williams, 1988), to complete at home and return to the OHS department for analysis. The results of both examinations to be available within the following three weeks, when the 'executive' returns for the full examination.

The examination is undertaken by one of the three doctors working within the York and Croydon OHS departments. The 'executive' completes a health screening questionnaire and has a resting ECG, audiogram, vitalograph and visual assessment performed. The attending doctor will then analyse the results of all the investigations with the person and offer suitable advice.

Results Management

It must be recognised that the handling of employee results is as important, if not more so, as performing the investigations. Care must be taken not to turn the 'well into the worried well'. The attending employee arrives feeling apprehensive but well, and should leave feeling reassured but with sufficient advice to make appropriate lifestyle changes.

During the initial implementation of the programme in 1989, the results of the screening procedure were discussed between the attending occupational health department professional and the employees, and they were then provided with general health education literature on weight reduction, smoking cessation, exercise, alcohol control, and so on as required. Consequently, some employees exited with several booklets to peruse—to be found at a later date within waste bins around the factory!

Following discussions between OHS staff, employees and health education professionals, an in-house results booklet was produced. This contains an explanatory note on why there is a need to perform the tests and individual pages on:

- Weight management and simple dietary advice
- Simple exercise programmes
- Smoking reduction/cessation
- Alcohol management

Within each section are written the individual's health screening results against what the 'normal' expected results should be, allowing simple comparisons and a basis for future results to be measured against.

No longer are these found in waste bins, as they have the individuals' names on the front cover and contain individualised advice. Indeed, many phone calls and letters have been received from employees' relatives thanking the company for simple advice that all the family can benefit from.

A resumé of the employees' results are sent to their general practitioners, once each individual's prior permission has been obtained. Collective summaries are produced on an annual basis for each site, providing that no named individual employee can be identified from the results. Analysis of the results has allowed monitoring and audit of the programmes and the development of appropriate intervention strategies. Active management by occupational health staff coupled with a wide awareness/education programme, employee peer pressure and a programme designed to meet both business and employee needs has led to a high uptake over the first three years.

Analysis of the Executive programme within the Nestlé Rowntree Division over the initial three years, demonstrates an active participation of employees and reduction in lifestyle risk factors (see Tables 3.2–3.4).

Table 3.2 *Attendance rates*

	1990	1991	1992
Eligible employees	185	182	178
Total screened	180	175	170
Percentage uptake	97.3%	96.2%	95.5%

Table 3.3 Cardio-vascular disease risk factor analysis

Risk factor	1990 (%)	1991 (%)	1992 (%)
Smokers	19	18	11.5
Taking regular exercise	38	53	55.5
Hypertension	5	0	0
Raised cholesterol	36	28	34
Overweight	36	31	32
Obese	5	4	3

Table 3.4 Attendances for general health screening programme 1990–1992 by location

Location	Males appointments	Males attending	% Attending	Females appointments	Females attending	% Attending
Location 1	136	126	92.65	373	339	91
Location 2	701	387	55.2	191	146	76.44
Location 3	52	45	86.5	4	3	75
Location 4	183	123	67.2	320	215	67.2
Location 5	528	437	83	1176	1043	88.7
Location 6	163	114	70	167	121	72.0
Location 7	484	320	66.1	418	340	81.4
Location 8	2658	1942	73.1	1173	900	77
Total	4905	3494	71.23	3822	3107	81.3

Total appointments offered 8727
Total attending   6601
Percentage attendance   75.64%

Analyses of employees' lifestyle-related health issues—weight, hypertension, smoking habits, alcohol intake, anaemia, raised cholesterol and lack of exercise—were in line with expected national measurements. Further evaluation of the general programme over the second three-year cycle will reveal whether employees have taken note of the programme results to individuals. Results from the 'executive' programme are already demonstrating changes in lifestyle which, if one believes that these changes will reduce risk of coronary heart disease, should lead to a reduction in mortality and morbidity.

The introduction of the Occupational Stress Indicator (OSI) into the Executive programme has had additional benefits. The majority of individuals within our society are happy to admit, and discuss, physical ill health but are reticent to admit to any sign of mental ill health. Such an illness is seen as a sign of weakness and will lead to stigmatisation for the rest of an individual's lifetime. With changes in society both at work and home, health-care professionals in all aspects of health care are witnessing increasing numbers of individuals with mental health problems. To manage such situations successfully within the work environment mental health problems need to be de-stigmatised and an increased awareness achieved.

Throughout any life there are only two certainties—LIFE and DEATH—and between these two points all individuals are susceptible to both physical and mental health problems depending upon particular circumstances and vulnerability, which are constantly undergoing change. The OSI allows an objective measure and understanding of the pressure/stress equation.

Each individual within the Executive programme is provided with a copy of the questionnaire to complete in the peace and quiet of home. The questionnaire asks the employee to answer questions on a range of issues on a scale of 1 to 6—issues addressed include:

- How do you feel about your job?
- Assessment of current state of health
- General behaviour
- Sources of pressure (job/home)
- Coping mechanisms employed

Upon receipt of the completed questionnaire the answers are programmed and an individual profile produced.

Discussions with the employee, following completion of the physical assessment, allow the individual to address the problems of 'pressure' and 'stress' and have increased the understanding of what pressure and 'stress' are, the positive effects of pressure, how the balance of pressure and stress can be regulated, how they can affect self and other individuals, how problems manifest themselves, how they can be recognised and can be addressed from a proactive standpoint. The OSI has done for mental health what the gamma GT has done for the 'problem drinker'—allowed individuals the ability to recognise the issues and to address them. Using serial questionnaires over three years, a profile can be produced allowing individuals to see how they are coping with issues and developing coping strategies for management. It has also allowed the OHS service to recognise issues occurring within areas of the business for which advice can be offered to management to reduce and manage health concerns.

POST-PROGRAMME MANAGEMENT

No health screening programme will be successful without follow-up and the development of intervention strategies. Where individual problems or concerns arise, individual employees are advised to visit their general practitioners and nursing staff will follow-up where required, to advise and encourage lifestyle changes. Many employees have undertaken changes in drinking and exercise habits, to include simple measures such as adopting one or two 'alcohol-free' days per week and using stairs instead of lifts, but many of the issues raised during the analysis had already been evident to employees but not actively addressed.

Recognising that the 'risk-factors' for coronary heart disease are lifestyle-related and largely under the control of individuals, there is a necessity to develop intervention strategies to encourage and assist employees to adopt change.

In line with the Occupational Health Service policy of continuing to evaluate OHS programmes in relation both to benefit to the business and employees and to cost-effectiveness, further changes were made during 1991 on the York site. Readers will recall that as part of the OHS resource via the York site there was a convalescent home at Scarborough—a legacy of the 1940s system of health care. With the increasing movement towards proactive health care and lifestyle management programmes usage of this was dropping and its cost-effectiveness being challenged.

A committee was formed comprising OHS staff, Union and employee representatives, and personnel management, chaired by the factory General Manager. Discussions continued over nine months to decide the best use of the resource to benefit as many employees within the site as possible. A decision was made to sell the convalescent home and by reallocating both capital and revenue resource a range of facilities were created, offering an increased range of benefits to include:

1 four convalescent stay beds at a Scarborough hotel;
2 the availability of counselling or in-patient care at a local psychiatric clinic;
3 the development of a weight watchers' programme
4 in-house physiotherapy service;
5 the development of an on-site fitness centre.

Weight Watchers' Programme

Accepting that carrying excess weight can contribute towards coronary heart disease, hypertension, osteo-arthritis and psycho-social concerns, employees wished to develop an intervention strategy to educate people and aid weight loss. The national organisation of Weight Watchers were contracted in to provide a series of courses consisting of a weekly 'weigh in' and lectures on diet and weight management, each lasting one hour, to be held on the company premises during lunch breaks. Throughout the first 12 months of the programme 130 employees attended and collectively lost 1200 lbs—an equivalent loss of 13 employees. Follow-up has demonstrated that the attending employees have maintained their weight loss.

Development of Physiotherapy/Fitness Centre

A review of NHS physiotherapy services within the vicinity of the York site demonstrated that any employee requiring physiotherapy treatment for musculo-skeletal problems could be waiting up to five months for a service, during which time their condition deteriorated, they and their families suffered pain and discomfort and the business was deprived of the employee's valuable services. A decision was taken to establish a service on site, as part of the OHS department, by utilising contracted-in physiotherapists in a purpose-built physiotherapy unit. All local general practitioners were informed of the service and to date 35% of referrals come directly from GPs. Waiting list times run at 4 to 5 days, benefiting both business and employee.

It appeared prudent to develop a fitness centre on a site of 4500 employees as part of the drive to reduce coronary heart disease and improve employee health (mental and physical). The service to be administered and monitored by the OHS physiotherapy service to provide experienced staff who could service a range of fitness and rehabilitation facilities. An area of the factory within close proximity to the OHS department was located and converted into a centre containing a reception area, changing and shower facilities, and testing and training areas which were equipped with a variety of strength and aerobic modules.

Strict control procedures are enforced in order to minimise risk to users—no employee being allowed to participate within the centre until they have undertaken an assessment programme during which an evaluation is made of the following criteria:

- Previous health problems
- Height/weight/body mass index
- Flexibility/suppleness
- Back and grip strength
- Stamina

The assessment is generated utilising the Fitech Body Management system, and results are fed into a computerised analysis programme which produces an individualised report and analysis. Upon completion the employee has an individualised fitness programme designed and is instructed in the correct use of all equipment and the procedures to be followed. Employees are allowed to attend the centre for a maximum of three one-hour sessions per week within their own time and to date 48% of a workforce of 4500 have attended.

The centre is open Monday to Friday from 07.30 until 20.30 and has a trained physiotherapist available for advice at all times—unsupervised training being strictly forbidden. Anticipated attendance expected a preponderance of males aged 20 to 35, but it was advertised on the basis of availability for both sexes and all age groups—Table 3.5 demonstrates the successful campaign designed to promote the message that fitness is everyone's right.

The assessment programme has also facilitated an on-going analysis of employee fitness issues, which are of use both to the individual and to the OHS department. Employees are encouraged to participate in reassessments and compare results to encourage on-going usage. Use of the facility remains high and it is encouraging to view employees of both sexes, all age groups, managers, process workers and union officials all exercising together. It has been the experience of the staff managing the facility that the success can be attributed to:

• The characters of the staff running the programme
• The professional approach and training of the fitness centre staff
• The marketing of the programmes
• The integration of the centre into health screening and physiotherapy services
• Availability of the facility within the workplace and accessibility
• The quality of programmes and mix of available equipment
• Commitment of the company to long-term health improvement

Future Developments

With the full integration of Rowntree Mackintosh into the Nestlé UK Ltd business, as created on 1 January 1992, a Nestlé UK Ltd Occupational Health Service was formed to create common standards and procedures throughout the business

Table 3.5 Employees attending fitness centre

Gender	Age groups					
	15–19 (%)	20–29 (%)	30–39 (%)	40–49 (%)	50–59 (%)	60+ (%)
Male	3	16.5	32	26	19	3.5
Female	4	22.5	20.5	24.5	16.5	2

available to all employees via 28 manufacturing sites and a series of distribution depots. Agreement was obtained that the voluntary health screening programme, so successfully implemented and managed throughout the Nestlé Rowntree factories, would be adopted at all locations to the same procedures and standards. This has required the creation of a standard procedures and quality control manual, the re-equipping of 14 sites with audiometers, vitalographs, keystone visual testing machines and desktop analysers. Occupational health staff from all locations have attended intensive training courses on the rationale behind the programme, procedures, equipment management, quality control procedures and delivery of results to employees.

Arrangements are in hand to provide a service to depots and sites where OHS departments are not available via a nurse attending with portable equipment. In order to inform and educate employees of the reasons for implementing the programme and the content, articles have been placed in the Company Newspaper, *Nestlé News*, and a video has been produced which is to be shown to employees at work.

A second fitness centre, based upon the format of the York success, is to be implemented within the Croydon head-quarters where 1200 employees spend several hours per day travelling to and from work, where they are all employed on sedentary jobs. It has been recognised by many of the nursing staff implementing the voluntary health screening programme that employees are presenting with problems and issues which require counselling. Problems which in many instances are not caused by work but which affect an employee's concentration, memory and dexterity and which could have an adverse affect upon the business. Effects upon an individual's safety, the safety of other employees, safety of product, attendance and absence and industrial relations problems are other obvious concerns. Nurses, and doctors, have little or no training in the counselling skills required to deal with these employee issues and, as a result, all nursing staff are to undertake a modular counselling programme developed in-house by trained coun-sellors who will also provide an on-going supervision and support service for those trained with counselling skills. A smoking at work policy has been developed and implemented and several sites are developing self-help groups to assist smokers in giving up the habit.

BENEFITS OF THE VOLUNTARY HEALTH SCREENING PROGRAMME

Many of the longer term health-related benefits will not be realised for many years if lifestyle changes do reduce the risk of coronary heart disease, but already the executive programme has shown that employees can be encouraged to take charge of their own health and make significant changes.

Short-term benefits for both the business and employees can be seen in the form of:

1 *Organisation*

- Promotion of the caring company approach
- Increased employee commitment and morale
- Better utilisation of OHS facilities
- OHS staff moving from reactive to proactive programmes and becoming multi-skilled practitioners
- Development of OHS policies related to hazard and risk with the development of specific surveillance programmes utilising the new equipment
- Ability to meet UK and EEC legal requirements on risk assessment and health surveillance
- Reduction in absenteeism
- OHS services being seen to be part of the business and contributing to productivity and profitability

2 *Employee benefits*

- Increased awareness of lifestyle-related risk factors
- Decreased ill health due to reduction in smoking and alcohol ingestion, dietary changes, counselling
- Family advice via health education material
- Reduced risk of accidents
- Availability of intervention facilities on site
- Commitment of the business to employee health issues

CONCLUSIONS

The Corporate Voluntary Health Screening Programme has been successfully developed, managed and integrated into a business structure to provide employees, managers and the business with an increased range and variety of occupational health services. It has facilitated the change from the reactive occupational health service of the past to the proactive position required for survival in the future. OHS staff have been developed into multi-skilled practitioners able to deal with business, legal and employee issues which have a direct bearing upon the health of individuals and the health of the business. OHS departments have been re-equipped to a high standard and appropriate training provided and quality control procedures implemented which have facilitated the development of surveillance and screening programmes to monitor employee work-related health hazards to meet business and employee needs. Occupational Health Services are contributing towards the reduction of employee health issues and the profitability of the business.

The success of the programmes can be attributed to:

1 Company commitment towards employee health issues.
2 Direct support from the Chairman and Management Committee for the development of the programmes.
3 Development of programmes which assist the business to meet its legal requirements, business needs and employee commitments.
4 An integrated business approach to the issues by the Occupational Health Service by understanding what the business requirements were.
5 Reviewing Occupational Health Service provisions in the light of a changing work/health environment and being prepared to adopt change in a cost-effective way without reducing efficiency.
6 Identifying programme requirements with care.
7 Identifying a programme manager, creating a strong team approach involving occupational health nursing staff, supporting administrative and secretarial services, physiotherapists and actively managing all programmes.

8 Developing and promoting an employee awareness programme.
9 Developing programme schedules, training and quality control programmes.
10 Developing a programme which is voluntary, free, in company time, confidential and accessible.
11 Developing an individualised approach with health education material containing simple advice directly related to the individual.
12 Auditing results to develop intervention strategies to assist employees take corrective actions to reduce risk.
13 Development of a positive attitude to auditing company health provisions with a view to change in the light of business or health changes and integrating the programmes within the company health and safety procedures framework.

It should also be strongly noted that these programmes were developed on the basis of an existing health and safety structure which is devoted to providing all employees with a safe and healthy work environment. Health surveillance programmes address the issues of hearing conservation and audiometry, lung function and dust exposures, safe driving of lift trucks, foodhandlers and hygiene, safe wearing of breathing apparatus and other programmes as identified via COSHH assessments. Without such a sound basis of health and safety no organisation should embark upon lifestyle programmes.

The Occupational Health Service of Nestlé UK Ltd watched with interest the launch of the 'Health of the Nation' white paper and the targets set to reduce the incidence of coronary heart disease, mental health problems, and other illnesses with reference to the workplace. These are targets and programmes which had been developing for three years within Nestlé UK Ltd.

In 1904 Rowntrees of York was one of the first companies to implement an Occupational Health Service and it has been recognised throughout the century for the development of employee programmes both within and outside the business. Once again developments within the company occupational health care service put Nestlé UK Ltd at the forefront of the proactive approach to health and safety which will lead to positive benefits for both business and employees.

REFERENCE

Cooper, C. L., Sloan, S. and Williams, S. (1988). *Occupational Stress Indicator: The Manual*. Windsor: NFER-Nelson.

4
Positive Mental and Physical Health Screening at Work

ROBERT WILLCOX
Group Medical Officer, Cable & Wireless

Grateful patients are few in preventive medicine where success is
marked by a non-event. (Rose, 1992).

Occupational Medicine has a strong history of a preventive
approach rather than the more traditional curative medical
model. The classic industrial example is of John Snow, taking
off the handle of the Broad Street pump in order to stop the
transmission of cholera in 1855. This bold initiative had a good
theoretical base but the benefit was not immediately obvious to
a considerably inconvenienced population. In the current
business climate with tightly managed resources, when justification of benefit is a regular exercise, a programme to change
lifestyles needs careful justification and promotion. The opportunity to introduce such a proactive programme arose in Cable
& Wireless in the early 1990s, and a highly focused programme
of work based on coronary risk and occupational stress was
begun. .

Creating Healthy Work Organizations. Edited by C. L. Cooper and S. Williams.
© 1994 John Wiley & Sons Ltd

SCREENING

Wilson and Junger first proposed their screening criteria in 1968, and they were postulated to apply to the broad range of medical conditions. They proposed that:

1 the condition should be important;
2 an accepted treatment must be available for the condition;
3 the facilities for diagnosis and treatment must be available;
4 a latent or early pre-symptomatic stage in the condition must exist;
5 a suitable screening test must be available;
6 the test/examination must be acceptable to the population;
7 the natural history of the condition must be understood;
8 an agreed treatment policy on whom to treat must exist;
9 the cost must be acceptable;
10 surveying must be a continuing process and not a once-for-all project.

Much debate surrounds the issue of coronary risk screening, chiefly on account of the relative contribution and importance of cholesterol among the various predisposing factors. But for coronary heart disease as a whole, it is clearly an important condition of mortality and morbidity in the Western world, and preventive action in smoking cessation, blood pressure control and treatment for very high cholesterol levels are available. Facilities for measurement and treatment are widely available. However, a latent or early pre-symptomatic stage is extremely difficult to define. Blood pressure and cholesterol measurement are easily available and widely acceptable. The basic outline of a natural history is still being formulated and debated. Treatment policy on blood pressure is widely accepted but there is considerable variation in approach to reduction in cholesterol levels. The screening costs have been found acceptable within a company context, and the surveying process is a continuing process, albeit with some debate on the interval between screenings.

Thus, the majority of the criteria could be met, and with conflicting media reports, a moderate balanced approach in which individuals could make a more informed decision on their lifestyle has been adopted in occupational health circles.

For occupational stress, the condition is certainly important both personally and corporately. Intervention studies are available, but tightly defined acceptable treatment is not yet formulated. Facilities for diagnosis and treatment are becoming more widely available. The continuous spectrum of stress makes a latent or early pre-symptomatic stage impossible to define. A variety of screening tests are available which are acceptable to the population. The natural history of the condition is increasingly well understood, both in medical and psychological terms. A treatment policy is difficult to define in such a diffuse condition. Acceptability of the cost of measurement depends on demonstrating the efficacy of an intervention, and this remains in a state of evolution. Stress measurement can be an on-going process.

This medical model of screening criteria with its emphasis on professional expertise in diagnosis, action and advice, focuses on the activity of the professional with his specific professional skills. In health promotion, however, any successful lifestyle programme must focus on on-going self-help and self-management. What brings real benefit depends on good factual presentation in an easily understood format. Considerable time and attention were paid to the motivation aspects of the screening programmes for coronary risk and occupational stress. The two programmes complement each other, not only by addressing both physical and psychological characteristics but also by having an easily understood numerical scale.

PREVENTIVE STRATEGIES

It has been argued cogently that we should be concerned with the whole spectrum of disease and ill health, 'because all levels are important to the people concerned and because the mild might be the father of the severe. The visible tip of the iceberg of disease can be neither understood nor properly controlled if it is thought to constitute the entire problem' (Rose, 1992).

There are two classical approaches to disease prevention. One either takes a population approach, where a small shift by the majority has a large effect, or a high risk approach, where one identifies a small number of people at the high risk end of the spectrum in whom a larger change can be effected. This may mean that one is only dealing with the margin of the problem.

Our approach to coronary risk and occupational stress contains elements of both strategies. Thus, for coronary risk, we sought a general lowering of cholesterol level among our employees, along with more targeted tuition for smokers and those with cholesterol levels above 7.8 mmols/litre. In occupational stress, our main approach was a population one, with general tuition given to all and only incidental extra tuition given to those at higher risk. Our emphasis in both areas has been on personal responsibility.

However, 'people are generally motivated only by the prospects of a benefit which is visible, early and likely. Health benefits rarely meet these criteria; they may be real, but they are likely to be delayed and to come to only a few of those who seek them' (Rose, 1992). With coronary risk, the motivating drive for change is an event which to many seems a long way off, although the financial advantage of smoking cessation is immediate and practical. In contrast, with occupational stress, although it may be more slippery to define, nevertheless, the possibility of change often seems more tangible and immediately beneficial. With these strategic principles in mind, our approach in using the Coronary Risk Profile and Occupational Stress Indicator will be described.

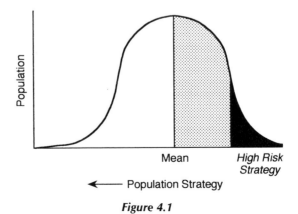

Figure 4.1

The Coronary Risk Profile

The coronary risk profile was designed primarily for use within general practice, although use within the hospital setting and occupational health was clearly possible (Tunstall-Pedoe, 1991). Of many risk factors, such as family history, exercise patterns, and so on, just three were capable of calculation of their relative contribution with reference to one another, and they were smoking, blood pressure and cholesterol. At consultation, a questionnaire was administered which covered smoking, alcohol consumption and exercise patterns. Cholesterol level was measured using a finger prick technique and a Reflotron Analyser (Boehringer). Height and weight were also measured. Calculation of risk was done using the standard risk disc and the results written on a sheet for the employee.

Individuals were placed in a queue of 100 people with 'one' at the front of the queue and a high risk for a coronary event, and a 'hundred' at the back of the queue with a low risk for a coronary event. Recalculation of the risk on smoking cessation or cholesterol reduction was achieved quickly and easily, being shown visually on the same sheet. This simple mechanism has had a very positive motivational effect in engendering change, particularly with smoking and nutrition. Giving authoritative figures relating to coronary risk was perceived as neither patronising nor preaching. The visual approach was particularly well received and it enabled the consultation to be deliberately brief, focusing on clear, easily understood information.

In particular the smokers, whose risk was usually poor, were able to grasp their risk more clearly and the implications of stopping smoking became particularly apparent as they moved up the queue. Those tempted to be neurotic about their cholesterol level were given a clearer perspective on what changes in their nutrition would actually achieve in terms of risk reduction This ranking approach to coronary risk fitted the underlined philosophy of our use of the Occupational Stress Indicator, which also gives measures that relate to the employee's stress experience, in a clear and quickly understood format.

STRESS FRAMEWORK

Mental attitudes influence a wide variety of health outcomes in the workplace (Creed, 1993). A working definition of stress isolates three key characteristics—that it is negative in quality, that it is personal to the individual (what one person sees as opportunity for job autonomy, another person may see as a situation of role ambiguity) and that it is a result of inadequate coping. Thus:

Occupational Stress is a negatively perceived quality which as a result of inadequate coping with sources of stress, has negative mental and physical ill health consequences.

The following working model encapsulates the relation between the multiplicity of stress sources and the influence of coping behaviour moderated around the fulcrum of personality, to produce effects either positive or negative.

The complexity of the interactions, and caution about the validation of any intervention, has historically meant only a guarded welcome by Occupational Health physicians. However, proactive occupational health includes preventive training of all employees in order to maintain and improve both

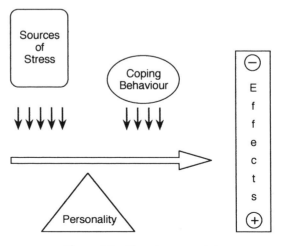

Figure 4.2 The stress model

individual health and the health of the organisation, and this must include mental health (Raffle, 1994).

Given the large part in our lives that the working environment plays in our mental well-being, both management and employees have a vested interest in optimising both conditions and skills. Issues of performance, morale and sickness absence are important for business success, and for many employees issues of personal growth and development are central to their personal sense of well-being and health. Thus, increasingly rigorous methodologies are beginning to clarify the issues of workplace stress in ways that lead to improved advice to both employees and management (Kasl & Cooper, 1987).

Previous research supports the view that at least 25% of the working population is psychologically stressed at any one time (Depue & Monroe Scott, 1986; Link & Dohrenwand, 1980), and many are characterised by a chronic pattern of disorder over many years (Hinkle, 1974). One survey of Society of Occupational Medicine members estimated that 45% of their managers suffered from some form of psycho-social stress (e.g. anxiety, psychosomatic illness, depression) (Cooper & Lawson, 1986). Perceived health ratings and mortality are related consistently, and in a manner that operates over time (Kaplan & Camacho, 1983). An improvement in mental health, particularly if sustained, would be most welcome both to management and to health professionals.

In an era of tightly managed resources when departments are lean, when targets are defined and effectiveness is measured, mechanisms for improving psychological well-being that are both efficient in their delivery and caring in their presentation are being explored in a variety of settings (Phelan, 1991; Fingret, 1984; Crossley, 1992).

The Occupational Stress Indicator

The OSI was developed by Cooper, Sloan and Williams in 1988, has been carefully validated (Robertson, Cooper & Williams, 1990; Cooper & Williams, 1991; Rees & Cooper, 1991), and has been used worldwide, covering Europe, the USA, Australasia, Hong Kong, China and the Pacific Rim. It consists of 167 questions which take about 45 minutes to answer at a computer terminal and which produce subscale scores under seven headings, with a score that relates to baseline UK data which include both blue- and white-collar workers.

Sources Of Stress	• Factors Intrinsic to the Job • The Managerial Role • Relationships with other People • Career and Achievement • Organisational Structure/Climate • Home/Work Interface
General Behaviour	• Attitude to Living • Style of Behaviour • Ambition
Total Type A Behaviour	
Events Around You	• Influence on Whole Company • Influence on Local Management • Individual or Personal Influence
Total Control or Influence	
Coping with Stress	• Social Strategies • Task Strategies • Emotional Detachment • Home and Work Relationship • Time Management • Involvement
Job Satisfaction	• Achievement/Value and Growth • The Job Itself • Company Organisational Design • Local Organisational Processes • Personal Relationships
Total Job Satisfaction	• Mental Health • Physical Health

The Consultation

Following completion of the disc, a personal consultation was offered to the majority (some received a group presentation to 5–12 employees). Both provided an opportunity for explanation and brief discussion. Each consultation started with an explanation that the scores were unlikely to reveal any surprises, that most people knew whether they were stressed or not, but that the clarity of the structure should enable them to focus on what they could or could not do. There was a firm statement that we were not counselling and that we were not going to be prescriptive, because we did not know the individual or their circumstances well enough to make good judgements with precise treatment. Rather it was a tool for individuals to use themselves.

The seven OSI scales were then explained briefly, followed by a comment on each individual subscale with its relation to any other subscale of particular relevance. Thus, the sources of pressure might be high, but if the coping skills were in place, it might simply mean a demanding job with which the individual was coping well. Very low pressure scores might mean that someone was bored and seriously understimulated.

Type A personality was briefly explained, with its component parts of attitude to living, behaviour and ambition. The interface between personality and influence scores was explored in areas such as the moderating of the medical ill effects of relative lack of influence by more Type B behaviour. Modification of Type A behaviour was suggested where appropriate.

Perceived lack of ability to influence managers was discussed, with the suggestion that this might need addressing with line management. Coping mechanisms were explained and the possibilities for improvement briefly outlined. Job satisfaction scores were also examined, and ways of improving them briefly explored.

The mental and physical health scores were explained, particularly the relation between mental health scores and psychosomatic symptoms. The mental health scores are derived from eighteen questions. The physical health scores are a measure of twelve symptoms which include headaches, indigestion, loss of libido, and so forth.

The final three subscales—job satisfaction, mental health and physical health scores—are the most useful ones, both in a short consultation and in longer counselling situations. Low scores for job satisfaction, whilst not invariably related to stress, are usually linked to high pressure. High scores for mental and physical health reflect high psychological morbidity and a high rate of psychosomatic symptomatology. When both mental and physical health scores are high, the physical symptoms may well be related to the high mental stress. In contrast, a high physical score but an average mental health score indicates that the physical symptoms are less likely to be related to workplace pressure. Detailed clinical work was not attempted in our brief consultation.

Use of OSI

Starting in January 1991, employees throughout the UK were invited by either phone or letter to participate on a voluntary basis. On acceptance of the invitation, a virus-free (checked) computerised disc questionnaire was sent, with operating instructions and an explanation card, specifying the appointment time. A general Health Check Questionnaire covering smoking, alcohol and exercise habits was also sent. The disc was completed at the employees' own terminal and brought to the consultation when the single page results were printed off and discussed, along with general health matters. A health booklet including a chapter on stress management was given out, together with an explanation sheet, to reinforce the tuition given.

From January 1992, some of the regional site visits were conducted with groups of 5–12 employees attending an interpretation session given by the doctor, and a brief individual consultation of five minutes to explore any personal issues. Two doctors and two nurses have been sufficiently trained to interpret the wide variety of results and to give a clear, concise assessment and consultation to employees for subsequent personal exploration of their own results. The style of presentation was very deliberately not a counselling session, but the focus was on giving employees the tools to manage their own workplace pressure. To our knowledge the brevity of this approach to using the OSI is unique, and thus we wished to explore the effectiveness of this intervention.

Intervention Study

From the population of 10 230, a group of 1283 were identified, who had completed a standard application of the OSI. All those seen since the inception of its use in January 1991 until July 1992, and who had not left the company, were identified in October 1992 at their current location, circulated with a second OSI computer disc and invited by letter on a voluntary basis to repeat the OSI with some additional questions (returning it to Occupational Health in a pre-paid envelope). A total of 1283 computer discs were circulated on 30 October 1992, and a single reminder telephone call was made during the five subsequent weeks. A second consultation was not offered, but the personal scores for both applications (OSI-1 and OSI-2) were sent to the employees with a repeat of the explanation sheet. Also included was the overall analysis of the first 629 received, with a comment on the overall company results.

The additional questions covered four main areas. Firstly, questions were asked about a change of job or a change within the same job. Secondly, employees were asked about any perceived modifications made in the light of the first OSI application, such as altered work patterns, behaviour, ambition, line management relationships, suggestions for job improvement made at work or attempts at home life improvement. Thirdly, a rating of the perceived helpfulness of the Indicator was addressed in six questions, and fourthly, a section looked at commuting patterns, perceived stress from the physical environment at work and the perceived possibilities for working from home.

By 7 December 1992, 654 discs had been returned and clean usable data produced from 615 responses. An OSI-1 leavers' file was compiled of those who had left the company (total 74—5.76%) and an OSI non-responders' file compiled of those not returning the OSI-2 disc by 7 December 1992 (total 629—49%).

Analysis was done by running subscale data against one determining question under the heading 'How do you rate the value of the Stress Indicator' which was:

Has your ability to address the issues of stress at work changed?

The focus of our interest was to maintain simplicity in choosing methods to answer four questions:

1   Did those with self-reported perceived improvement start with different demographic or stress profiles?
2   In those with self-reported perceived improvement, what measures in the OSI have they used to achieve change?
3   Did those who failed to respond to the OSI-2 invitation have a different OSI-1 profile?
4   Did those who left the company have a different stress profile from those who stayed?

The mean scores in OSI-1, OSI-2, and answers to additional questions were compared in those able to improve ('improvers') and those not able to improve ('non-improvers') with a test on the difference. Further analysis compared mean OSI-1 scores in those who responded to the invitation to complete a second OSI ('responders') and those who declined the invitation ('non-responders'). And finally, mean OSI-1 scores of those who had perceived improvement in their ability to address stress issues at work ('improvers') were compared with OSI-scores of those who had left the company ('leavers').

Results

Of 615 analysable responses to the question:

Has your ability to address the issues of stress at work changed?

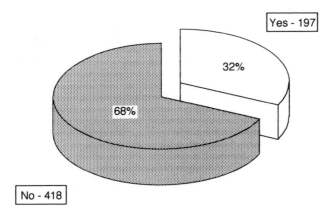

Yes - 197

32%

68%

No - 418

Figure 4.3

Figure 4.4 shows the change in scores between the first and second application of the OSI, highlighting the differences between the 'improvers' and 'non-improvers'.

DISCUSSION

Longitudinal study in a fast-changing corporate environment is not easy, particularly when a myriad of factors may affect psychological features in the workplace, but there is increasing investigation of the importance of subjective accounts of health in monitoring medical outcomes (Kind & Carr-Hill, 1987; Jenkinson, Coulter & Wright, 1993).

The Occupational Stress Indicator is a well-validated tool, giving reproducible broad measures of mental and physical well-being. The proposition in this study was that a brief consultation in which the clarity of the OSI structure was allowed to speak for itself, engendering personal ownership of the problems and personal responsibility for the solutions, should in itself result in an improvement in the baseline subscales (Shipley & Orlans, 1988). The results showed that those individuals who believed that after completing OSI-1 they had increased their ability to manage stress ('improvers') scored significantly differently in all stress subscales as well as job satisfaction, mental and physical health subscales, than the 'non-improvers'.

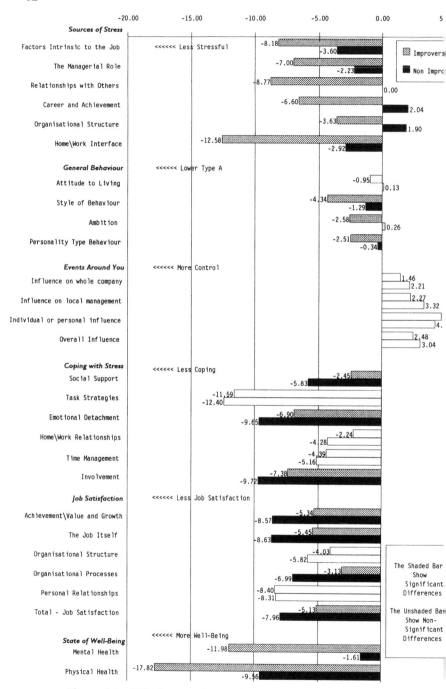

Figure 4.4 *OSI change (OSI-2–OSI-1 intervention analysis)*

Demographic Features

The 'improver' and 'non-improver' groups showed no significant difference in the distribution between men and women, of age or of the four job categories. Thus, ability to learn and improve was not related to sex, seniority or age. These features were of no value for targeting those likely to improve nor for disqualifying those unlikely to benefit from the OSI.

The time interval between OSI applications which varied from 61 days to 681 days did not influence the changes. This implied that the learning process was sustained through the period of study, with a representative number of those with a long time interval being able to maintain the improvements made. The mean time interval for both 'improvers' and 'non-improvers' was 336 days.

Measures of Improvement Used

Modifying Sources of Stress

The 199 'improvers' started from a position of higher occupational pressure and higher Type 'A' behaviour, which may be because they had chosen more stressful jobs. There is some evidence that high-strivers (with 'magnificent obsessions') have higher psycho-social stress than the lower-strivers (with 'trivial pursuits') and less physical ill health (Emmons, 1992). In this study, the 'improvers' were able to moderate their stress levels and their Type A behaviour, as well as improving their physical health scores.

The data suggest that a significant number of 'improvers' addressed their stress problems by changing jobs into a less pressurised environment. They moderated their Type A personality significantly compared with 'non-improvers', and chose paths which provoked less stress. The highly significant reduction in every stress subscale suggested that improved understanding led to practical action. Thus, apart from any job change, they changed the intrinsic pressure areas and their personal responses in terms of behaviour and ambition. They started from a position of higher stress, where they were more in need of change and more able to change. It is possible that their higher Type A behaviour made it more likely for them to perceive the need to change (Robbins, Spence & Clark, 1991).

Consciousness—raising the issues in those who were highly stressed—led to an improvement rather than a deterioration in scores, even without detailed personal counselling on what measures to take. The 'people' pressure decreased, which was matched by an improvement in social strategies and emotional detachment. The career pressure decreased, which was matched by a reduction in ambition (Beehr & Newman, 1973). These improvements were achieved following application and feedback of the OSI results, with only a brief explanation.

Modifying Influence and Control

The 'improvers' were just as lacking in managerial and organisational influence and control as the 'non-improvers', except they were significantly more in control in their personal work sphere. This could imply that they were more likely to be concerned with doing the job well, and more ready to take measures to that end than the 'non-improvers'. The pattern of control showed significant deterioration between the two applications which reflected a perceived increasing impotence in the face of workplace dynamics. Of particular interest is the fact that the 'improver' group changed many features of their stress profile, but they were not able to change their overall influence (locus of control) scores. This was despite the fact that the 'improver' group perceived 'discussions with management' as significantly more useful, along with more positive attitudes and response to suggested job improvements. The likely conclusion is that there was a short-term effect on perceived control, which did not influence the workplace reality in the longer term. It seems that the more personal issues were addressed (e.g. home—work interface) and personal influence rather than the issues of workplace politics.

Modifying Coping Skills

Coping skills deteriorated markedly through the period of study. However, the decline was significantly less marked in the 'improvers' in social strategies, emotional detachment and involvement. In the face of deteriorating social strategies, the relative moderation of loss of social strategies may well match their change in personality type (moderation of Type A behaviour), and be linked with tuition on the pitfalls of a 'macho' management or interpersonal style, which does not make the best use of collaboration with colleagues.

The period under study was one when many of the goal posts were redrawn and *emotional detachment* was often difficult to maintain in practice. Against such a background both social strategies and emotional detachment were important skills to retain, and the 'improver' group was more effective in doing so.

Very significant deterioration in *task strategies*, associated with a marked deterioration in their downward personal influence, suggested that both 'improvers' and 'non-improvers' were unable to improve their personal control by operating more effectively. It would seem that being more organised (task strategies) was not seen as a fruitful way of addressing the problems. Significantly less deterioration in *involvement* in the 'improvers' suggested that they were less inclined to walk away from the problems and more likely to engage the difficulties.

In the majority of studies, coping is strongly related to cognitive appraisal (Folman & Lazarus, 1986). In this study, a substantially maintained repertoire of coping skills was clearly a positive benefit, but not sufficient to explain markedly improved mental and physical health scores.

Modifying Job Satisfaction

Marked deterioration in job satisfaction in both 'improver' and 'non-improver' groups was significantly softened in the 'improver' group in four subscales. Less deterioration in achievement, value and growth could imply a more realistic attitude which may match the moderated Type A behaviour. More realistic expectations of the job may have been induced by the OSI application.

Interestingly, there was no difference in 'improver' and 'non-improver' groups in the drift in satisfaction in organisational structure ('the politics of the workplace'), but the *day-to-day processes* were significantly better maintained by the 'improvers'. This confirms that the application of the OSI influenced more local, personal areas rather than the wider issues in workplace life. The popular notion of making an organisation flatter and less hierarchical may tend to benefit those who are able to modify stress by addressing more immediate personal issues rather than organisational issues.

The 'improver' group started by gaining more satisfaction from personal relationships than the 'non-improvers'. Also they alleviated their *people stress* score more than the 'non-improvers'. This, coupled with significantly less deterioration in social strategies, suggested that the 'improver' group was better able to learn to modify the people elements of workplace stress.

Overall, the OSI application significantly ameliorated the drift in job satisfaction in those who perceived an enhancement in their ability to address the stress issues. During the study there was a significant steady deterioration of job satisfaction scores on OSI-1. The general consensus within the organisation was that the period of exceptional growth, with three major reorganisations in seven years and the uncertainty consequent on so much change, was close to the heart of the reason for such increasing job dissatisfaction.

Modifying Mental and Physical Health

Both groups improved their mental and physical well-being, but strikingly more successfully in the 'improver' group. The mechanism for this effect is related to the observed stress reduction rather than improved coping or improved job satisfaction, neither of which occurred. It suggests that mental and physical well-being can be improved by disengagement from the workplace problems, as opposed to addressing them more effectively. It seems that rather than attempting to improve job satisfaction, many 'switched off' as a protective mechanism, leading to improved mental and physical health scores. This 'switching-off' process was significantly curtailed in the 'improvers' whose better scores than the 'non-improvers' probably represent a balance of mixed methods—both more effective engagement and more appropriate disengagement.

No measures of workplace performance were available with which to correlate during this period. No sickness absence data were collected for the same period, but given that at least 30% sickness absence has a strong mental morbidity component (Jenkins & Coney, 1992; Nicholson & Johns, 1985), it is possible that the OSI application could play a role in reducing sickness absence.

The Non-responder Profile

Stress research always has difficulty in producing an adequate control group. It was judged unethical and impractical to administer the OSI to a group without giving them the results (Wald, 1993). There were no significant demographic differences or differences in OSI-1 between the 'responders' and 'non-responders', which strongly confirmed that the study population was not a biased one. There was no evidence that the 'responders' were more stressed and potentially either more keen to achieve change or more cynical about the ability to change. On the other hand, neither were they less stressed and therefore not perceiving any value in responding to the invitation.

The unanswered question that remains is whether there is a 'spontaneous remission' rate (i.e. improvement without intervention). However, the validity of the intervention results is strengthened by having no significant differences in the initial subscales of the 'non-responder' and 'responder' populations.

The Leaver Profile

The leaving or turnover rate was 5.76% in the study group, compared with 7.80% in the company as a whole during the same period. The fact that the 'leavers' were significantly more stressed was hardly surprising, but it is important to note that they were only more significantly stressed than the 'improver' group in the *career and organisation* subscales. Not surprisingly, the 'leavers' were also younger (mean age 'leavers'—32.89 years, 'non-leavers'—37.50 years). They also showed significantly more Type A behaviour than the study population as a whole, but not more than the 'improver' group.

A key difference between the 'leaver' and 'improver' group was that the 'leavers' felt relatively impotent to influence the company as a whole and unable to change that situation, a feature which was likely to be related to their departure.

Significantly greater *social support* and *involvement* coping strategies in the 'leavers' suggested that they had invested heavily emotionally in their local personal workplace surroundings, which contrasted with their feelings of relative impotence to influence the wider company. In spite of being more involved in the job, their satisfaction scores were all significantly worse, which mirrors poorer mental and physical health scores. Thus, the response under pressure was either to leave or to change. The emerging pattern was of three groups with increasing pressure (Figure 4.5).

It was clear that the 'improvers' were a group who were helped to address the problems rather than leave. Dissatisfaction with 'career progress' and with 'the organisational structure' was a marker of those who benefited least from this application of the OSI, and whose best option was to leave. The data neither support nor refute the contention that the OSI application prompted employees to leave, although the

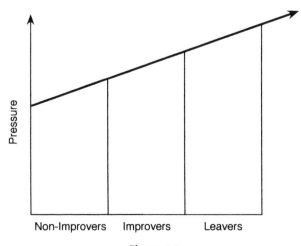

Figure 4.5

production of objective dissatisfaction scores well validated against the general population was likely to have provoked a serious review by those with low scores.

CONCLUSION

During the period of study, in the population as a whole, mental health and physical health improved whilst workplace pressure was reduced. This was against a background of deteriorating job satisfaction, no significant change in personality, little improvement in influence or control at work or in coping skills. The most likely explanation was a disengagement from the workplace, as a result of three fundamental restructuring exercises in the organisations.

Within this picture, a third of the employees assessed responded to the OSI by perceiving it to have enhanced their ability to address stress issues. They reduced their stress scores by moderating their Type A behaviour, significantly stopping the slide in the use of three coping skills and the slide in job satisfaction scores. Improved understanding in this 32% of employees led to a highly significant improvement in health outcomes from a brief intervention, and this was achieved by addressing the more personal issues rather than the organisational structural issues. Thus, the OSI was a useful diagnostic tool leading to appropriate personal action, but more advice on organisational issues for management is required to provide a fully-rounded approach.

The data also highlighted the fact that perceived 'openness with senior management' did not lead to any improvement in 'perceived ability to influence'. Managers still need to learn the lessons of empowerment, and occupational physicians can facilitate that process with validated data and health-promoting advice (Walker, 1993).

Our experience has shown the OSI to be a helpful diagnostic tool for individuals, and our 'initial' use of it has given us a sufficient base from which to give accurate and apt advice, both to individual employees and to management, to create an increasingly healthy organisation. It is clear that for individuals,

70

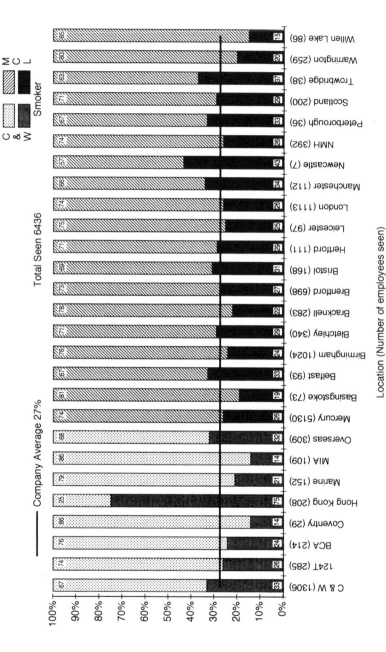

Figure 4.6 Occupational health—Smoking, 20 September 1993

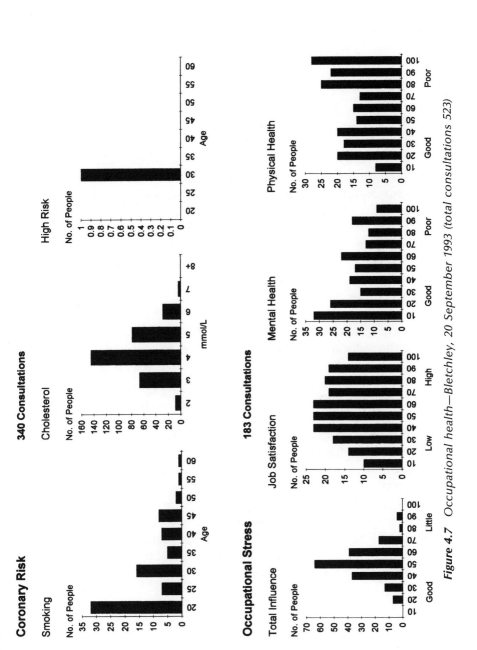

Figure 4.7 Occupational health—Bletchley, 20 September 1993 (total consultations 523)

awareness is half the solution. The same may well be true for management.

FURTHER DEVELOPMENT

Our strong approach to clear information and personal responsibility focused initially on individuals and then explored group presentations. Collating and presenting the data to management was the next phase, being careful to maintain individuals' confidentiality and analysing the data to identify the practical measures that management could take. A company-wide eight-page document called *Picture of Health* (Figure 4.6), covering coronary risk and occupational stress in all locations, was discussed with local management, so that they could compare their results with other areas. A single sheet to illustrate their local features was then produced (see Figure 4.7).

Two other programmes are being developed under the title 'Focus Fitness'. In conjunction with Moorfields, we have developed a visual acuity test on the laptop computer along with a motion sensitivity test to screen for glaucoma. In conjunction with NASA (Houston, Texas), we have developed a fitness assessment without the need to exercise (Jackson, Blair, Mahar et al., 1990). This is based on the same visual principle as the coronary risk profile. Our chief aim is to motivate the majority to undertake a little more exercise rather than to cater for those who are already very fit.

Both screening programmes meet the basic criteria for medical acceptability and the bottom line criteria set by management. There is very broad welcome for this attempt at 'health by design', although, to date, we have been precluded from calling it it 'Blood, Sweat and Tears'! Our consistent theme is personal ownership of the problems and personal responsibility for the solutions.

REFERENCES

Beehr, T. A. & Newman, J. E. (1973). Job stress, employee health and organisational effectiveness. A facet analysis model and literature review. *Personnel Psychology*, **31**, 665–699.

Cooper, C. L. & Lawson, G. (1986). A survey of stress at work. *Society of Occupational Medicine*, **36**, 71–72.

Cooper, C. L. & Williams, J. (1991). A validation study of the OSI on a blue-collar sample. *Stress Medicine*, **7**, 109–112.

Creed, F. (1993). Mental health problems at work. *British Medical Journal*, **306**, 1082–1083.

Crossley, D., Myres, M. P. & Wilkinson, G. (1992). Assessment of psychological care in general practice. *British Medical Journal*, **305**, 1333–1336.

Depue, R. A. & Monroe Scott, M. (1986). Conceptualisation and measurement of human disorder in life stress research: The problem of chronic disturbance. *Psychological Bulletin*, **99**, 1, 136–151.

Emmons, R. A. (1992). Abstract versus concrete goals: Personal striving level, physical illness, and psychological well-being. *Journal of Personality and Social Psychology*, **62**, 5, 753–759.

Fingret, A. (1984). Responding to change: The view of a company doctor. *J. Roy. Coll. Physicians*, **18**, 3, 172–175.

Folman, S. & Lazarus, R. S. (1986). Dynamics of a stressful encounter: Cognitive appraisal, coping and encounter outcomes. *Journal of Personality and Social Psychology*, **50**, 5, 992–1003.

Hinkle, L. E. Jr (1974). The effects of exposure to culture change, social change and changes in interpersonal relationships on health. In B. S. Dohrenwand and B. P. Dohrenwand (eds), *Stressful Life Events: Their Nature and Effects* (pp. 9–44). New York: Wiley.

Jackson, A. S., Blair, S. N., Mahar, M. T., Wier, L. T., Ross, R.M. & Stuteville, J. E. (1990). Prediction of functional aerobic capacity without exercise testing. *Medicine and Science in Sports and Exercise*, **22**, 6, 863–870.

Jenkins, R. & Coney, N. (eds) (1992). Prevention of mental ill-health at work. A conference. London: HMSO.

Jenkinson, C., Coulter, A. & Wright, L. (1993). Short form 36 (SF36) health survey questionnaire: Normative data for adults of working age. *British Medical Journal*, **306**, 1437–1440.

Kaplan, G. A. & Camacho, T. (1983). Perceived health and mortality: A nine year follow-up of the human laboratory cohort. *American Journal of Epidemiology*, **117**, 3, 292–304.

Kasl, S. V. & Cooper, C. L. (eds) (1987). *Stress and Health: Issues in Research Methodology*, New York: Wiley.

Kind, P. & Carr-Hill, R. (1987). The Nottingham Health profile: A useful tool for epidemiologists? *Soc. Sci. Med.*, **25**, 905–910.

Link, B. & Dohrenwand, B. P. (1980). Formulation of hypotheses about the true prevalence of demoralisation in the United States. In B. P. Dohrenwand, B. S. Dohrenwand, M. S. Gould, B. Link, R.

Neugebauer, & R. Wursch-Hizrig (eds), *Mental Illness in the United States: Epidemiological Estimates* (pp. 114–132). New York: Praeger.

Nicholson, M. & Johns, G. (1985). The absence culture and the psychological contract—who's in control of absence? *Academy Management Review*, **10**, 397–407.

Phelan, J. (1991). Work stress, family stress, and depression in professional and managerial employees. *Psychol. Med.*, **21**, 999–1012.

Raffle, P. A. B., Adams, P., Baxter, P. & Lea, W. R. (eds) (1994). *Hunter's Diseases of Occupation*, 8th edn. London: Edward Arnold.

Rees, D. W. & Cooper, C. L. (1991). A criterion-oriented validation study of the OSI outcome measures on a sample of health service employees. *Stress Medicine*, **7**, 125–127.

Robbins, A. S., Spence, J. T. & Clark, H. (1991). Psychological determinants of health and performance: The tangled web of desirable and undesirable characteristics. *Journal of Personality and Social Psychology*, **61**, 5, 755–765.

Robertson, I. T., Cooper, C. L. & Williams, J. (1990). The validity of the occupational stress indicator. *Work and Stress*, **4**, 1, 29–39.

Rose, G. (1992). *The Strategy of Preventive Medicine*. Oxford: Oxford University Press.

Shipley, P. & Orlans, V. (1988). Stress research: An interventionist perspective. In J. J. Hurrel, L. R. Murphy, S. L. Sauter & C. L. Cooper (eds), *Occupational Stress Issues and Developments in Research*, London: Taylor & Francis.

Tunstall-Pedoe, H. (1991). The Dundee coronary risk-disk for management of change in risk factors. *British Medical Journal*, **303**, 744–747.

Wald, N. (1993). Ethical issues in randomised prevention trials. *British Medical Journal*, **306**, 563–565.

Walker, M. C. P. (1993). Occupational health—a manager's view: A discussion paper. *J. of Roy. Soc. Med.*, **86**, 35–38.

5
Company Alcohol Policies: Practicalities and Problems

DAVID A. MOORE
Director, Group Medical Services,
Scottish & Newcastle plc, Edinburgh

INTRODUCTION

Alcohol and work. This has always been an uneasy relationship. Genius may be fired by wine. More commonplace talent is often fired because of it. At one time the rationale for dismissal may have been moral delinquency. Today it is usually poor job performance, misdemeanour or exasperation with the sheer organisational nuisance the persistent alcohol misuser too often represents. Of course, in dismissing such an employee the employing company is tacitly admitting failure: failure to act early enough to prevent a problem becoming a crisis; failure to conserve valuable resources of manpower and management time; and failure to ensure the well-being of its employees as far as it is reasonably able.

But for more than half a century there has been a rather better way of doing things: the Company Policy on Alcohol. Pioneered by the DuPont Nemours Corporation in 1942, the policy is in essence little more than a formal undertaking by the employer to guarantee 'treatment', a qualified freedom from

Creating Healthy Work Organizations. Edited by C. L. Cooper and S. Williams.
© 1994 John Wiley & Sons Ltd

disciplinary action and job security to the repentant drinker. In the past two decades in particular, the concept has been marketed actively to industry and commerce (usually in association with offers of training and 'treatment' services) by a variety of commercial, public and charitable agencies. Despite —or perhaps because of—its empiricism, it has been widely adopted by a large number of companies of very different character. In many ways, it has become accepted as one of the signs of the progressive and enlightened employer—it is 'doing the decent thing'. But just how effective is it? How good is the average policy on alcohol? How easy is it to operate? Does it do any more than improve the corporate image?

The answers to these questions lie not only in the policy itself, but in the actions and reactions of the companies that adopt it, in their structures and management systems and, particularly, in their people. In this chapter, the introduction and operation of a policy on alcohol is examined within this setting, with the purpose of illustrating some aspects of the reality of policy performance in industry in contrast to the sometimes rather propagandist claims made by some protagonists, particularly the crudest claim that an alcohol policy will solve all your alcohol problems. The illustration will be based upon experience acquired from the 'inside' from work in the field in two large companies (one of them a brewer), both operating a policy on alcohol, and from the 'outside', from work with Councils on Alcohol, particularly in the area of provision of workplace policies.

Like all experience, this is a mixture of the general and the particular. The general should be modestly useful to most readers; the particular, by its very nature not directly transferable, may still be of some value in the quantification rather than qualification of the difficulties and successes to be expected in the operation of a policy. It is to be hoped that the two will not be too hard to distinguish.

MOTIVATION AND OBJECTIVES

In any enterprise, it is instructive to examine the motivation for and to identify the objectives of any policy innovation.

Experience suggests that in the adoption of a Policy on Alcohol as a company policy, most companies have decidedly mixed motives and few have clear objectives.

Motivation normally comes from within the company. This being so, and dependent upon the company, it may have philosophical, paternal, disciplinary, financial or self-publicising elements, usually with one of these considerations being dominant but rarely with any of them being absent. Its expression, both inside the company and in the company's external relations, may primarily be explicit or implicit. Given its complexity, however, it is usual to find that some elements are made explicit and some are not. This is not to say that companies necessarily have a 'hidden agenda'—in this respect they are usually insufficiently self-aware to think of one—but expression is usually a faithful reflection of the company's self-image and helps to explain the sharp differences in attitude and method that may be seen by the interested observer from company to company. What is less obvious and much more important is that, because of existing preconceptions and most companies' lack of real knowledge and experience of the subject, motivation is influenced more by perception than reality, specifically by industrial and public relations perception and stereotypical views of alcohol misuse.

Such motivational complexity inevitably affects vision, and it is hardly surprising that companies and their managers lack clarity in their objectives. Indeed, to the outside agency 'selling' the policy, there often appears to be a passivity about the whole process that suggests more a begrudging management acquiescence in the proposal than active involvement. It is rare for the agency to see anything resembling a tender document or, indeed, anything that tells it exactly what the company expects and what the company intends to achieve.

Why do normally competent managers when faced with a fairly straightforward innovation (the policy on alcohol) not only fail, but do not even try to identify an objective? As has already been suggested, it may be no more than a reflection of their lack of faith in the 'concept' being capable of delivering the goods—but if this is true, why do it at all? Even where objectives have been identified, they are too often unrealistically optimistic or expressed in vague or expansive terms. What are the reasons for this? They are not wholly motivational, although they may share some of the causes of the mixture of motivational factors referred to above, particularly those that are internally generated. Few companies have any idea how large or important their problem is with alcohol misuse, partly because it is very rare for them to have even looked, and partly because alcohol abuse is notoriously hard to define. It is understandable that managers feel uneasy with issues of uncertain magnitude that lack satisfactory definition, particularly if they lie outside their area of competence, and it is not altogether surprising if their stated objectives bear little relation to what could be reasonably expected. No one takes too much trouble to define a result that he or she does not expect to achieve.

This difficulty apart, the management team may be misled by the selling agency. Few workers in these agencies have any experience of management, particularly outside the public or voluntary sectors. The organisation and execution of management projects in the private sector with its relative lack of bureaucracy, its time pressure and its extreme resource sensitivity, may be a mystery to them.

Mixed motives and absent or hazy objectives are not a promising starting point for a successful policy initiative. Even if the will is there, most companies have, as we have seen, little knowledge or experience of the manifestations of alcohol misuse, its occupational, social and domestic effects, or of the availability and quality of the providing agencies and their facilities for its 'treatment'. As indicated above, many of the agencies promoting policies on alcohol to companies have little knowledge or experience of commerce and industry, the complexities of company structures, the politics of corporate management and employee relations. The difficulty the company may have in the definition of objectives and decision making is, therefore, often compounded by a lack of mutual comprehension and common perception when the introduction of a policy is being negotiated with the providing agency. There is, therefore, a hiatus of conception, perception and communication that neither side can fill easily, but more importantly, of which neither side might be wholly aware or prepared to acknowledge. This is a serious matter. It carries a considerable risk of mistake and waste of resources—mainly money and time—and an acute risk of the destruction of employees' confidence in the good intentions of the management. A muddled introduction of a policy on alcohol, which in theory at least is designed to safeguard health and employment, can be construed by employees as being a further device available to management for discipline and dismissal.

There are other dangers. Without common ground and mutual understanding, either side (employer or agency) may give assurances in good faith that in reality will be extremely difficult to satisfy, not only in the sense of fulfilment of contract but also with respect to the amount of time and money that will be necessary to make the policy work. The company may not realise, and in time may find insupportable, the resource demands prosecution of a policy will make upon its management team. The providing agency may find itself being 'sucked in' and involved in complexities of company management systems and employee relations that are quite beyond its capabilities. It is not unknown for assurances to be given in bad faith. As already indicated, the company might want a policy for no other reason than to appear 'progressive' or to sweeten employee relations, and could have little intention of devoting the time and resources needed to make it work. The agency may be merely money-spinning; selling a paper policy with no real intention, or perhaps lacking even the capability of providing any structured assistance to the customer to make the concept live. At its worst, therefore, all that takes place is the mutual transfer of pieces of paper; one bearing an outline policy, the other the rubric 'I promise to pay the Bearer on demand'.

Objectives are usually matched by expectations of results. For the reasons advanced above with respect to objectives, companies adopting a policy will often have quite naïve and unrealistic expectations of the likely result. Bad as this is, the situation can be worsened where, as sometimes happens, the alcohol policy is taken up as a 'cause' by some influential member of the management team. The adoption of a policy may be marketed to the rest of the company as the ultimate solution to a longstanding and intractable problem. Moreover, in the solution of this problem the company (and by implication, the managers involved) can be seen to be on the side of the angels—a rather uncommon position in the experience of most employees. The enthusiast may evangelise (this term is not used loosely) his colleagues, and a wholly uncritical implementation of a policy might follow. In circumstances where enthusiasm is allowed to obscure prudence and reason, inflated expectations are almost certain to be dashed. Resource demands too may be found quite surprising when related to the doubtful benefit such ill-considered action may bring. Finally, uncritical and ill-thought through policy introduction can lead to the disaster of the discreditation of the whole concept in that particular company, much to its own detriment and very much to the detriment of the individual employee with an alcohol misuse problem.

In conclusion, experience suggests that it is only in those companies where the introduction of an alcohol policy is subject to the same disciplines of thought and planning that would be applied in the case of any other policy, where results in line with expectations are likely to be achieved, some cost benefit identified and employees in trouble given help.

POLICY OWNERSHIP

Probably three out of four policies on alcohol fail within a year or two. This is not because the concept is faulty, but is nearly always because no one in the company makes it work. This is not necessarily a matter of idleness or incompetence: it is usually because no one feels sufficiently responsible for the policy, no one 'owns' it in any real sense. As we have already seen, it is only too easy to acquire a ready-made policy from some outside agency, retype and issue it, and that sometimes this is done cynically to help erect a façade of the caring employer. Much more often it is due to inexperience, haste or plain carelessness—or, unfortunately, a management view that a policy on alcohol is of little importance. Whatever the reason, it is this lack of a sense of ownership that leads to failure, and if the company's management team has not been involved in policy formulation, development and training they are always likely to regard the policy as someone else's responsibility. It could be argued that this 'naturalisation' of the policy represents needless reworking of principles that are simple and clear. But this is not so. It differs in no way from a company's response to, for example, new legislation. The law is the same for everybody, but each company makes its own policies to satisfy it and make it conform to that company's style. Even more importantly, the procedures that are the only mechanism by which the policy can be executed must be developed by the company—no external agency can do it. These procedures are not easy to devise. They may impinge upon several other areas of company policy and procedure, and there may be mutual incompatibilities that will require resolution.

Within a company there might be some doubt as to which management team should be responsible for the policy on alcohol. In all but the smallest organisation, it should be a responsibility of the personnel function, but where companies have occupational health staff the temptation is always to 'medicalise' it. Why? The usual reason given is that alcohol misuse is a medical condition. It is not—although it may certainly cause ill health. Another reason, although rarely acknowledged, is that it is 'difficult' and therefore properly is to be left to the experts—but doctors and nurses are not expert in this field, unless they have been specifically trained for it. It *is* difficult, but there are at least three good reasons why it should not be medicalised. The first is that, whether it is hard or not, formulation and execution of company policy is a prime management responsibility. The second is that to medicalise the policy is, in most companies, almost certainly to marginalise it. Finally, as stated above, the best reason not to medicalise the policy is that there is very little that is medical about it. It is not a policy on the treatment of cirrhosis of the liver or delirium tremens, it is a policy on the management of what is primarily a behavioural problem within the company. This is not to say that certain responsibilities under the policy may not be delegated to an occupational health department, but management involvement in and responsibility for the policy must continue.

Another potential problem, particularly with small companies, arises in letting the selling agency introduce and conduct the policy on the company's behalf. There are obvious attractions in a 'turnkey' project that the small and inexperienced (at least in this respect) company would find hard to resist. The danger is that mentioned above: neither side is likely to know the other's methods, organisation or capabilities, and it is a hazardous business indeed to allow one organisation to determine procedures for another. The result can be serious employee relations difficulties, confusion and the risk of the destruction of mutual confidence both between the company and its employees and between the company and the agency.

It is stating the obvious, but there is no substitute for commitment and hard work. In any company of any size, an alcohol policy will only work if managers themselves have the will and energy to make it do so.

TRADE UNION INVOLVEMENT

Policies on alcohol clearly fall within the field of employee relations and are a legitimate matter of employee representative interest both in their formulation and in their operation. Indeed, in some companies, the initiative to introduce a policy may well come from a trade union representative. Because companies, trade unions and their respective relationships vary so widely, it is not possible here to be dogmatic on this aspect of policy introduction, but it would be a foolish management that attempted to introduce a policy to a unionised workforce without at least trade union acquiescence. Once the policy has been introduced, and if it is operated with the proper degree of confidentiality, it should not feature largely in management–union exchanges. It should not be forgotten either that the policy applies to the individual manager as much as it does to the shopfloor worker (see below), and both sides therefore have a vested interest in seeing that its operation is fair and efficient.

GETTING THE RIGHT POLICY

This might be better expressed as getting the policy right. As discussed already the typical policy on alcohol is simple and the principles can be expressed as follows:

1 The policy applies to all employees equally, irrespective of grade.
2 Affected employees are entitled to:

(a) 'treatment';
(b) time off for treatment, with normal company sickness benefit;
(c) security of employment;
(d) immunity from alcohol-related offence discipline.

3 Registration and treatment under the policy is confidential

Although requiring a number of supporting administrative procedures to make it work, this paradigm appears to be quite reasonable. Indeed, it is based upon a policy version issued by an agency well respected in the field, and adopted by at least one major corporation. It identifies the drinking employee's rights under the policy, and guarantees even-handedness of treatment from the shopfloor to the boardroom, all in confidence. It does have one embarrassing drawback. It provides an almost perfect cover for the drinker to continue to drink with impunity. In fact, once accepted under this policy, the drinker is fireproof. The term is used advisedly: Fireproof, Not Dismissible. As it stands the policy imposes neither duty nor any need for remedial action on the drinking employee. There is no mutual commitment and no contract. There must be more, there must be a basis of contract between the employee and the employer with a clear statement of mutual rights and duties. Without this contract trust is difficult to establish, and without trust, no policy on alcohol will work. The statement 'immunity from alcohol-related discipline' must be qualified as below.
Unless

• The drinking employee refuses to acknowledge the existence of an alcohol problem.
• Refuses advice or treatment.
• Fails to comply with advice or treatment.
• Fails to respond to or benefit from advice or treatment.

These qualifying statements are frankly coercional, and there is little doubt that some people will feel uncomfortable with them, perhaps on vaguely liberal grounds or, more likely, because they recognise the potential for difficulty in employee relations. Disregarding the first, which is a matter for individual opinion, the second must be addressed. The fundamental basis of industrial relations law is 'fairness'. In this respect, fairness must lie in the way the policy is applied. The policy itself to some extent establishes this principle in that it explicitly requires equality of application, irrespective of grade. But this is not enough. There must be consistency of application. There must be a detailed procedure governing the operation of the policy that is comprehensive, fair, written down and observed in every case. This procedure must define the action to be taken in all foreseeable eventualities. Obvious questions that must be answered unequivocally in a standard written procedure include:

- What is a 'drinking employee'?
- Who is to identify the drinking employee?
- What criteria are to be used?
- How is referral for help to be carried out?
- Is clear distinction made between 'disciplinary' referral of an employee by his manager, and self-referral?
- To whom is referral to be made?
- How is employee refusal of referral to be handled?
- Who (if anybody) needs to be informed?
- How often and by what means are they to be informed?
- How much are they to be told?
- How is the drinking employee to be 'registered' under the policy?
- How is employee refusal of registration to be handled?
- How is he to be 'signed off' as 'cured'?
- What documentation is to be used?
- Who is to have access to and be responsible for it?
- How is trivial relapse to be handled?
- In the event of serious relapse after treatment and successful 'cure' how much time (if any) must elapse before readmission to the policy register is permitted?
- Who is to be informed of the employee's condition or progress?

- Where employees are self-referred under the policy and are subsequently subject to discipline with an alcohol-related offence, how and in what circumstances can confidentiality be broken so that they may claim protection under the terms of the policy?
- What is to happen if the employee fails to keep his part of the contract?
- Who makes the decision that the employee has indeed failed?
- What action are they to take?
- How are employees to be informed of their rights and duties under the policy?
- What are they to be told?
- Who is to tell them?

Here are twenty-five questions, and the list is not exhaustive. Logical, fair and comprehensive answers must be found to them. The procedure is as important as the policy itself, and is, regrettably, often never written down or, worse, once written is neglected by managers for many of the reasons given above concerning motivation and ownership. The potential for unfair treatment of employees and corresponding employee relations difficulties is self-evident.

PUBLICITY, EDUCATION AND 'AWARENESS'

Policy and procedures are central to the control of alcohol misuse in a company. What is nearly as important, and what can certainly be as critical for success, is the presentation of the policy and procedures, both externally and internally. Here the management enthusiast, already mentioned above, may cause serious difficulty if allowed to operate unchecked. Characteristically, this enthusiast not only wants to save the drinker from him or herself, but simultaneously wants to make certain that the company gets the maximum credit for being so 'enlightened' as to adopt so 'progressive' a policy to achieve this end. This is not a cynical observation. The only sensible basis on which a company should adopt a policy on alcohol is that of enlightened self-interest; however, we are dealing here with problems of means rather than ends and practicality rather than rhetoric is needed. But if the rhetorical and self-advertising mode is adopted, there is room for understandable but serious error that can be illustrated by the experience of one major company. In this company, the enthusiasts (who had no special knowledge and very little experience of work in this field) pursued a high profile public relations campaign, with what was then an unusual and sensitive acknowledgement that there was a widespread problem of alcohol misuse within the company and, what was even more unusual, that they intended to do something about it. This message was given to all who would listen through presentations, media interviews and newspaper articles. They made it clear that what they were going to do not only included the establishment of a policy on alcohol but also the initiation of a large, complex and expensive research project in conjunction with an eminent research body. This research project was intended to provide an evaluation through mass screening of employees, by determining the prevalent level of alcohol misuse and monitoring the effect (if any) of the operation of the policy. As expected, the company gained credit for this initiative, and for a while was the cynosure of its sector—at least in this respect. Unfortunately little thought appeared to have been given to the effect of this publicity upon the employees, who after all were the people most nearly affected. The result was predictable. Many employees reasoned that if the company was making all this fuss and spending all this money, there must be a problem— and they were it! The impression was gained that the company thought its employees a bunch of boozers. An unfortunate turn of phrase from one of the enthusiasts, picked up at an inter-view and reported in a local newspaper, confirmed the impres-sion. Worse was to follow. The researchers, who had carried out what proved to be a quite invasive mass screening exercise on a large number of employees, had promised individual health status 'feedback' to participants. This of course was the main incentive to employees to participate in the survey. No such feedback was received.

The overall result of this well-meaning, but ultimately disastrous, PR exercise was that employee confidence in management goodwill was damaged and confidence in the policy as a means to help those in trouble fell very low. Of course, it was not quite so simple. This was a new initiative and like all such was therefore a subject of suspicion. The stigma of alcohol misuse and the threat it represented to security of employment, meant that there was inevitably a great deal of defensiveness and collective denial among employees. This was ironical in that the very purpose of the policy was to avoid stigma and possible job loss. With the benefit of hindsight, it can now be seen that the damage was done in trying to extract favourable public opinion advantage for the company (and, dare one say it, for the enthusiasts), from what should have been a carefully thought through policy introduction in what was inevitably a sensitive area of employee relations. The resultant damage to employee confidence set back the successful prosecution of the policy by several years.

The sad thing was that the company really was enlightened, well-meaning and one of the first in the field. What a pity to spoil it.

Internal presentation of the policy and procedures to employees can also present problems, particularly if there is confusion over aims, the message and the nature of the audience. These problems may occur even where the company is experienced in employee communication and employs managers who are normally competent in the field.

Dealing with aims first, it is surprising how even here, there is failure to distinguish between the separate requirements to provide information and to influence attitudes. The usual thing is for there to be an attempt to do both together, usually to their common detriment. The message too can be made incomprehensible by the confusion of aims and a desire to get every possible piece of information into the presentation. Finally, there may be little effort made to define appropriate presentations and presentation styles for different audiences. These problems are hardly unique to the subject of alcohol policies. They do, however, appear to be more prevalent in this field. This may be due to a general managerial lack of confidence in their ability to deal with what they persist in seeing as a specialist or expert subject. In the company referred to above, the exercise was carried out in a highly didactic manner that bore more than a little resemblance to Sunday School. One presentation package was expected both to inform and to influence attitudes of employees at all levels and in all areas of the company. It did not work very well.

Experience shows (again, hardly originally) that the message must be kept simple and while groups may be informed it is only worth trying to influence attitudes with individuals. The message is simply:

- What constitutes harmful drinking?
- What does the policy on alcohol say?
- How does the employee take advantage of it?

To inform, this message may be delivered to groups of employees as a straightforward statement of fact. To influence attitudes it should be delivered to individuals in a confidential and personalised way on an 'opportunity' basis. This can be done in the course of interview or management counselling by managers, particularly personnel managers or, where the company has an occupational health service, by health professionals at pre-employment medical examination, health screening or counselling. However, and by whoever this work is done, whether informing or influencing attitudes, it must continue indefinitely. It is quite useless to introduce a policy on alcohol and rest content with a single cross-sectional briefing exercise.

The target of this work, the audience, is 'all employees'. All need the basic information. Many of them would benefit from a change of attitude. Managers need this and much more. Managers need to understand the policy and its systems. They need instruction in the handling of their employees with a drink problem. They need training in the recognition of employee or performance problems that may be drink-related. This is often by no means easy. Most of all managers need to be given the confidence to use the policy to manage the situation.

Attitudes have already been mentioned. They are of course enormously important and notoriously difficult to change. In the field of company alcohol policy implementation, it is helpful to consider attitudes as falling into two groups, that for convenience might be called 'internal' and 'external' attitudes.

'Internal' attitudes underlie the defensiveness, denial and guilt so often associated with alcohol, whether or not the individual has a problem. 'External' attitudes underlie the reaction of one individual to another with a drink problem; a reaction that may vary from being censorious to being protective. The distinction between 'internal' and 'external' may be psychologically naïve but experience shows it to have practical value. Trying to make 'internal' attitudes constructive is important for all employees, irrespective of grade. Trying to make 'external' attitudes constructive and indeed consonant with policy objectives is absolutely vital for managers. Problems with these sets of attitudes are at the root of many of the practical problems now to be described.

PEOPLE PROBLEMS

It is a truism to say that all company policies, however well designed and however well supported by procedures, will work only as well as people are prepared to make or allow them to. With no policy is this more true than with a policy on alcohol. Alcohol consumption is an intensely personal matter and, disregarding for the moment self-referral, all alcohol policies hinge upon the detection of the problem drinkers who have neither the insight nor any motivation to volunteer themselves for help. In other words, who points the finger? Theoretically, in a company with a well designed policy, good procedures, and where both employees and managers have been trained, nothing could be easier. After all, most problem drinkers are far from adept in concealing the fact (although some are), and to people trained just to think about alcohol as a cause for poor work, absenteeism, bad behaviour and social and domestic difficulties, problem drinkers tend to stand out rather clearly. Unfortunately, attitudes get in the way. The peers of the problem drinker at work are generally reluctant to say or do anything, either because of a somewhat misplaced loyalty or, what is more likely, a natural unwillingness to interfere in an area of behaviour that is seen (and in most circumstances, quite properly) as a private matter. It is hard to criticise this restraint. A work community where workers watched each other and were prepared to denounce aberration would be quite unacceptable in our society. Sometimes this reluctance is carried too far. It is not responsible behaviour for a lorry driver's mate to fail to report the driver's drunkenness. Nevertheless, experience shows that in the operation of a policy on alcohol little can be expected from the colleagues and workmates of the drinking employee.

What about managers? In dealing with their subordinates they are not subject to the constraints of peer relationships, and it is their clear duty to manage their area of responsibility, including the people, as efficiently as possible. Do they actively identify potential problem drinkers in their area in conformance with their own policy procedures? Experience suggests that sometimes they do, but nearly always too late. Detection and referral is too often a crisis action rather than a preventive one. It is worth looking at the reasons for this observation. The first is that managers share in full measure that reluctance to 'interfere' in what is seen to be a private and personal matter as described above. This is understandable, although in a manager somewhat reprehensible. The second reason is even less creditable. Confronting an employee with the news that he or she may have an alcohol problem is not easy—particularly if the manager has been 'winking' at the individual's alcohol-related work problems for months or years. Even the efficient, conscientious manager, prepared to take action without delay, may be daunted by the potential for employee relations difficulties, by consciousness of perceptual differences, in particular in the definition of an alcohol-related work problem, by actual differences in age, sex and experience and, very often, by contrary precedent (the manager's predecessor not being efficient, conscientious, etc.). The fact that the alcohol policy with its procedures is designed to deal with these very difficulties is forgotten. It is just too easy to put off action, usually in the vain hope that the problem will solve itself. Of course it may, but it may also worsen, seriously affecting work and too often giving the employee enough rope to hang him or herself.

People problems that will be very familiar to occupational health staff who give service in support of an alcohol policy, are manipulation and duplicity by managers. One of the commonest manifestations of this is the referral of a drinking employee, not under the terms of the company's alcohol policy but bearing a medical label. Typically, the manager, who has known perfectly well that Jimmy has been a 'soak' for years and has sailed as close to the wind of dismissal for as long, will refer him to Occupational Health. He arrives complete with a spurious diagnosis, a domestic hard luck story and a sickness absence record going back five years and illustrating his repeated bouts of 'gastro-enteritis', 'nervous debility', 'dyspepsia', 'depression', 'ulcers', 'neurasthenia' and so on. The accompanying memo will outline Jimmy's difficulty in managing to do his job, the manager's difficulties in getting the work done with Jimmy's absences and inefficiencies (due entirely to his medical condition of course), the impossibility of redeployment to another job and, finally, the hint that a recommendation to the pension fund trustees that Jimmy be retired on grounds of his health would be most welcome. Typically again, this manager is well aware of the alcohol policy and its provisions. His real problem is of course that he either cannot or does not dare to summon up the hardihood to challenge the man and refer him properly under the terms of the policy.

Timewasting is also a problem with some managers. There are those who enthusiastically embrace the alcohol policy in principle, are rather less keen to have their subordinate management staff appropriately trained, and find it quite impossible to release their shopfloor workers to attend alcohol education sessions. There is then a total inertia as far as alcohol referrals are concerned. The object of these managers is of course to get the credit without doing the work or committing the resources, and it is a departmental vice paralleling that of whole companies referred to earlier.

Manipulation, duplicity and timewasting are the stock-in-trade of many drinking employees, although by no means all. Experience suggests that the dull, the arrogant, the insightless, the devious and the dishonest are mixed in roughly even numbers with the genuinely suffering, the motivated, the constructive and the honest. They can make the manager's task very difficult even with the support of good procedures under the policy. From an occupational health perspective, the satisfaction that may be felt in helping the genuinely suffering is finely balanced by the sinking feeling when Bill turns up with another infantile excuse or George breathes whisky all over the room while swearing with bare-faced mendacity that he has not touched a drop for weeks.

DIAGNOSIS AND TREATMENT

'Diagnosis' and 'treatment' are words with a strong medical connotation. 'Diagnosis' in this instance does have its medical meaning, although it is not necessarily carried out by a doctor or nurse. 'Treatment' is used as a shorthand to describe the whole range of helping strategies available.

It is self-evident that if the problem drinker at work is to be helped under the terms of a policy on alcohol, the condition must be diagnosed; the diagnosis should not only identify but as far as possible highlight its principal manifestations and say something about its degree of severity. Fairness demands and experience illustrates the need for the diagnosis to be competently made and as reliable as possible. It is not unusual for a person to refer themselves for help under the alcohol policy in circumstances where alcohol is not the source of the difficulty, and may indeed not be involved at all—sometimes an excessively tender conscience (or an excessively intolerant spouse) has been the reason for seeking help. It is also not unusual for managers to refer employees in the mistaken belief that they are misusing alcohol These people may or may not need help, but if they do it is not for their drinking.

Simple diagnosis apart, the degree of severity of the alcohol problem must be determined. There is a spectrum of alcohol abuse, and the drinking employee needs placing in it. There is a world of difference between the treatment needed for a physically dependent and perhaps physically damaged drinker, and that for the person who has misused alcohol sufficiently to have acquired a range of employment and domestic problems but is personally well-preserved.

The importance of diagnosis is such that it must be carried out by those who are competent to do so and not by the referring manager. In this a good Occupational Health Department is very useful in that the occupational physician or nurse will normally have the skill and experience to make at least a provisional diagnosis, and know where to refer the employee and whom to consult. Companies without Occupational Health Departments would be well advised to make arrangements for advice and consultation either with a local doctor, preferably one with occupational health experience or qualifications, or directly with one of the providing agencies referred to above. In the latter case a member of management staff should be identified to establish and maintain liaison with the agency and, if possible, undergo some basic training from them.

There is a wide array of treatment services available. This in itself may cause confusion but some clarification is possible. The physically dependent drinker, who surprisingly perhaps is often still in work, needs thorough clinical assessment at a hospital unit (not necessarily as an in-patient) where physical damage can be investigated and treated, drying-out expertly supervised and where longer term support can be arranged. In industry, these people represent a tiny minority of problem-drinking employees. Choice of treatment for the rest is not so easy. There are not only different treatment agencies but different agencies support differing therapeutic concepts. Some agencies demand abstinence on the part of the drinker, some accept 'controlled' drinking. Some additionally have strong religious overtones. Some agencies provide help to individuals only, others only to groups, others still to both. It is sometimes difficult to make a choice, but in general it is best to suit the drinking employee to the agency that is likely to be most congenial to him or her. This is not merely a matter of being kind to the individual, since it has real therapeutic value in itself. Some people, for example, will really be helped by the certainties of abstinence, fellow sufferer support and maybe public personal catharsis offered by Alcoholics Anonymous. Others would rather die than make so overt a declaration of their troubles, but may find confidential counselling, being gently guided through the maze of difficulties and not being threatened with the loss of their social life through complete abstinence, both congenial and effective. Still others may be better suited by group therapy, with abstinence or controlled drinking as options rather than absolutes. All of these treatments work on some people. None of them work on everybody. They are not even mutually exclusive, although it would not usually be sensible to have an employee attend two agencies at once.

Alcoholics Anonymous has been mentioned already. The other major source of assistance is the countrywide network of Councils on Alcohol. These organisations are charities and are staffed (in the main) by volunteers who are formally trained in alcohol counselling. They do not usually charge directly for their services, but are always grateful for corporate or individual donations. They specialise in one-to-one counselling and in some places group counselling. Most large towns and cities have NHS alcohol or addiction treatment services manned by psychiatrists, psychologists and psychiatric nurses. Finally, there are numerous private agencies offering a variety of treatments according to a variety of treatment theories. NHS facilities are of course free and, apart from treatment for the physically dependent referred to above, provide group therapy and some other services. In most towns they are attached to the local psychiatric hospital. This may cause difficulty as to some people attendance at such a centre would involve stigma and the mere fact of referral may be seen as threatening or even insulting. The private agencies include those that are based in country houses and are perceived by many people as being for the very rich or for those who wish to hide themselves away while they take the 'cure'. These prejudices are not always justified, but country house treatment, however good, is almost always very expensive and outside the reach of the average employee.

Experience suggests that the Councils on Alcohol provide the best general purpose treatment for the drinking employee, where best can be defined in terms of accessibility, acceptability, cost and effectiveness.

CONFIDENTIALITY

In this account confidentiality has been mentioned but not stressed. It is now the place to do so. It is impossible to overemphasise its centrality in the successful operation of a policy on alcohol. It is important not only because there is a moral and ethical duty to maintain it but because without it no policy will work. Most people are ashamed of alcohol misuse. Those who are not are probably so insightless that they are past help, at least while their state of mind persists. Failures of confidentiality are usually due to faults or omissions in the policy's supporting procedures, or to carelessness or malice. There is no excuse for the first two of these, and it is apparent that if they are avoided there is little opportunity for the last.

The real reward for the confidential operation of the policy is that drinkers begin to refer themselves long before they get to the stage of insoluble or irrevocable employment or domestic difficulties. This is the ultimate policy objective.

WHY BOTHER?

This has been an account of the pitfalls and problems of operating a policy on alcohol. They are many and various, and the reader could be forgiven for coming to the conclusion at the head of this section. But no one said it was easy—and if they do they are not to be believed. There is no doubt, however, that a properly designed and executed policy on alcohol will work. It will help solve some intractable management problems, and it does give a company an opportunity to help some of its employees very much to both their and the company's benefit.

6
Developing a Company Mental Health Plan

ANN FINGRET
Consultant Physician in Charge, Occupational
Medicine, Royal Marsden Hospital, London and Surrey

INTRODUCTION

The cost of mental health problems to industry is enormous. The Confederation of British Industry has estimated that the annual cost of sickness absence certified as being due to stress or mental disorder is in the order of £5.3 billion (Banham, 1992). The Health and Safety Executive has suggested that 80 million working days are lost due to mental illness each year. These figures of course relate only to absences labelled as being due to mental illness. It is acknowledged that many more absences, though carrying physical illness labels, are in fact related to lack of mental well-being. Probably even more damaging to business efficiency is the situation where the employee is at work but is not performing satisfactorily. Occupational Health practitioners and psychologists are well aware of significant levels of stress and psychological maladjustment which have not resulted in significant sickness absence. The Health of the Nation Document (HMSO, 1992)

Creating Healthy Work Organizations. Edited by C. L. Cooper and S. Williams.
© 1994 John Wiley & Sons Ltd

singled out mental health as one of the key areas that needed to be addressed to enhance the nation's health.

Psychological illness and psychological health are concepts which seem difficult for the average employer to define and comprehend. Even in occupational health circles where the concept of health rests on the International Labour Organisation's definition, 'The highest degree of physical, mental and social well-being', practitioners have been slow to address anything other than hazards to physical health.

There is also a resistance by employers to addressing the issue because there is still a belief that whereas an employer has a responsibility to protect and promote the physical health of employees, psychological health is the responsibility of the individual. The legal situation is in fact quite different.

LEGISLATION

The first cohesive framework for health safety and welfare at work was the Health and Safety at Work Act (HMSO, 1974), and its associated regulations. This Act required all organisations employing more than five staff to produce a policy statement on health, safety and welfare. Some of the more enlightened employers included a reference to mental health in this statement. However, in most organisations the statement amounts to nothing more than a commitment to physical safety.

More recently promulgated law stemming from EEC health and safety legislation, namely the so-called 'six pack', has further defined and extended employer and employee responsibilities. The Management of Health and Safety at Work Regulations (HMSO, 1992) require employers to list and assess all workplace hazards. This provides another opportunity for employers to acknowledge organisational and interpersonal relationship problems as definable hazards. It should, of course, be more than an opportunity because it is a mandatory requirement. However, it may be difficult for a manager to acknowledge that working in his department is not good for the psychological well-being of his staff! One would hope that at the very least this would be recognised as a hazard in work areas which are known to be associated with a greater risk of psychological trauma, such as emergency services and health care work. The impact of change on psychological well-being is also well documented and at times of change this should be recognised as a controllable hazard.

COMMITMENT TO HEALTH

The foundation stone for an organisational mental health policy should be the health, safety and welfare policy statement signed by the Chief Executive. This must include a reference to the promotion and maintenance of both physical and mental health. To ensure that this overall commitment to employees' health is implemented a comprehensive health plan should be developed. It may be necessary to persuade employers that this holistic approach to health is the one most likely to maintain an efficient workforce. Even when a real commitment to health has been made by managers and endorsed by the unions and the workforce, the objectives and expectations of each group may differ widely. The priorities as seen by occupational health departments may be different again.

An organisation's commitment to health has to encompass not only the stated intention to enhance employee health and an implementation plan but also the provision of resources to carry this forward. This does require some vision because the cost–benefit equation has yet to be clearly demonstrated. The expected outcomes of initiatives aimed at improving the mental health of staff, such as improved performance, commitment, job satisfaction, and reduced sickness absence, are not easy to measure. Several large companies in North America such as Du Pont (Bertera, 1990) and Johnson and Johnson [Jones, Bly & Richardson, 1990] which have mounted workplace health interventions have shown decreased levels of sickness absence of up to 29%. There have been few audited studies in the UK, but there seems little reason to suppose that there would be a different outcome.

Any Health Plan needs to include initiatives for both individual and organisational health. To date the emphasis has been very much on the individual, not least because initiatives to help individuals are easier to mount and are certainly less expensive.

DEVELOPMENT OF THE PLAN

There are four stages in the development of the Health Plan:

- Assessment
- Production of plan
- Implementation
- Feedback

To ensure ownership at an early stage, a small working party should be set up. This should include a committed line manager, a union representative, a human resource manager, an occupational health and safety adviser and, if not one of the above, the individual who will undertake the assessment. It cannot be emphasised too strongly how important it is to have senior management involved at this stage. The working party will be responsible for receiving the assessment, developing the plan and producing a plan for implementation. It will also ensure communication on progress to all parts of the organisation.

Assessment

In order to develop a comprehensive plan for employee health, it is necessary to look at the existing organisational structure and culture. Some aspects of organisations have been identified as relating to the level of psychological health among employees (Cox & Kuk, 1992). These are shown in Table 6.1. Information on these and other relevant organisational factors will be obtained in the assessment. The assessment will also provide information on the needs of the organisation. It is probably best undertaken by someone trained in occupational medicine or psychology. The assessment will cover a number of areas.

Table 6.1 *Factors relating to the experience of workplace stress*

Organisational culture
Management and Social Environment
Communication
Task Environment
Problem-solving Environment
Staff Development Environment

Source: T. Cox & G. Kuk (1992). Healthiness of schools as organisations: Teacher stress and health. *Proceedings of the International Congress on Stress, Anxiety and Emotional Disorders*, University of Minho, Portugal.

The Organisation

1 What is the organisational structure?
2 What is the organisational culture—e.g. caring, macho, etc.?
3 What is the communication structure?
4 Are communications perceived to be good by managers and by the workforce?
5 Does the Health Safety and Welfare Policy include a reference to mental health?
6 Are organisational changes underway or planned?
7 Does any level or any part of the organisation perceive itself to be particularly under pressure?
8 What arrangements are there for problem solving?
9 Is management really committed to developing a health plan—what do they believe this to be?
10 Are the unions really committed to a health plan? What do they believe this to be?
11 What order of resource is likely to be made available for the implementation of the Health Plan?
12 Are sickness absence or staff turnover rates high? Is this a stable state?
13 Are there any other indications of low staff morale?
14 Does the organisation appear to be in 'good health' to the employees and to the general public?

Human Resource Management

Role

1 What is the role of this function? Is it simply management of resources or does it also include pastoral care?

Policies

1 Which health-related policies are already in existence, e.g. alcohol/smoking?
2 Is there an equal opportunity policy?
3 Is there any positive or negative discrimination for groups covered by equal opportunities legislation?
4 What is the normal retirement age? Does it vary for different groups of workers?
5 Are there restrictions for entry into the pension fund?
6 Are most posts permanent or short-term contracts?
7 What is the annual leave entitlement? Is it the same for all staff?

Recruitment procedures

1 What is the current mode of selection?
2 Is health one of the criteria for selection? What procedure is used?

Sickness absence

1 Is there any formal procedure for monitoring sickness absence?
2 Are there any sickness absence statistics? Are they expressed solely in resource management terms or for epidemiological purposes?
3 What is the sick pay entitlement? Is it the same for all groups of staff?
4 What is the organisation's approach to temporary light work or other forms of modified duties?

Termination on the grounds of ill health—medical retirement

1 What are the organisation's rules on superannuation and early retirement?
2 How flexible is the organisation in the application of these rules?
3 What is the role of the organisation's medical adviser?

Nature of work

1 Are there jobs with special physical or psychological requirements?
2 Are there jobs with known physical, chemical, biological or psychological hazards?
3 What are the patterns of work? If there are shifts, how satisfactory are they in relation to employee health?

Safety management

1 Are safety professionals employed? If so, what is the thrust of their activities?
2 What is the relationship between safety and occupational health?
3 In general are there well-defined policies and safe working procedures? Are these audited? How well are they adhered to?
4 Is there a safety management structure?
5 Is there a consultative structure?

Occupational health structure

1 How many occupational health staff are employed by the organisation? What are their qualifications?
2 Are there external occupational health or occupational health-related advisers? What are their qualifications?
3 To whom does the senior occupational health adviser report?
4 Are counsellors or other psychological support staff employed?

5 What is the present cost of occupational health or health promotion/protection activity on a per capita basis?
6 If there is no occupational health input what is the source of health advice?

Training

1 Is there a training department?
2 Are all staff included in staff development programmes? How extensive are these?
3 What aspects of health education are included in the general training programme?
4 Is occupational health involved in general training programmes such as management of change and stress management?

THE MENTAL HEALTH PLAN

The assessment period may take some time, particularly if it is carried out by an external occupational medical or psychological consultant. Time taken here, however, is worthwhile as initial ideas can be tested out at later meetings and in group discussions. It is very important not to form opinions too soon and to listen to the 'the music behind the words'.

The assessment should provide a clear picture of the organisation's structure, culture and procedures. Procedures already in place which address the mental health needs of staff will have been identified as will areas where there is a need for further development. The mental health plan will include all these aspects, but the implementation programme should take account of what is already in place. The core of the plan covers the four areas shown in Table 6.2 and described below in detail.

Table 6.2 *Core areas of mental health plan*

Improving the Person/Job Fit
Improving the Organisational Style
Development of Health-related Policies
Development of Staff Support Systems

Improving the Person/Job Fit

Personnel Selection Procedures

The assessment will have highlighted both good and bad selection procedures. These are often a matter of custom and their efficacy will need to be established. It goes without saying that there are 'horses for courses' and that the right person in the right job is a recipe for both individual and organisational well-being. Normally the method used is comparative selection for rejection or acceptance. However, it may be very difficult to ensure a person/job fit. For most jobs the profile of the perfect employee has not been defined. There is conflicting evidence on the success of pre-employment psychological testing. A good test should be well validated and should measure effectively what it is supposed to measure although, as already stated, there may be no clear definition of what the employer is looking for. A psychological test may also be used to predict behavioural patterns. Many of the tests used analyse the personality of the individual. Such tests are used more commonly in management appointments and in the appointment of individuals to organisations with relatively clear personality requirements such as police forces. Information on more controlled trials in the use of personality tests does not seem to be forthcoming. At best these tests should only be used as an adjunct to good interviewing techniques. A good interview should at least give the opportunity to assess whether the applicant would fit the style of the organisation.

The Plan should address the issue of personnel selection. This will include:

• Identifying areas where psychological testing might be appropriate
• Assessing the validity of current selection procedures
• Assessing the competence and training of those required to select personnel

Training

To maximise employees' effectiveness training is essential.

There should be well-designed training programmes for staff at all levels. These will cover various areas:

Ability to do the job. Deficiencies in the person/job fit can be minimised by adequate training. Employees' training needs should be assessed and organised on appointment and on a regular basis. The plan should include training programmes for posts and for individuals.

Lifeskills training. The workforce is a 'captive' audience for this type of health promotion activity. To be effective the message will need to be repeated in different ways. This should be available for all members of staff. Such training allows individuals to understand what are healthy choices for physical and mental health, it enables them to express their views in an assertive way, to manage their time effectively, and to understand the dynamics of relationships. This sort of training is probably most effective in workshop form. Individual training linked to fitness assessment can be useful particularly in the area of lifestyle but it is generally an expensive use of specialist resources.

A detailed health promotion programme should be part of the plan. However, unlike job skills training, participation is voluntary and a variety of initiatives will be needed to maximise the effect of these activities.

Management training. The ability to manage does not come naturally. There are still many managers who have received no training in the management of people. The skills of good management are easy to define (Table 6.3) but difficult to practise. The specialist nature of work today means that most managers have risen up a professional or technical line. Their managerial role requirement gradually overtakes in importance

Table 6.3 *Good management*

Regular/Open Communication
Being Able to Delegate
Being Able to make Decisions
Fair Criticism
Fair Appraisal

their professional or technical role. Well-balanced communication with their own staff may be difficult to achieve, leading to either overindulgence or apparent indifference. Good staff appraisal systems are relatively rare and yet regular constructive appraisal is a very significant part of job satisfaction.

There should be no exception to the principle of training in the fundamental elements of good management for anyone placed in a management position. The plan should contain a comprehensive training programme.

Training to manage stress. The plethora of courses and books on stress emphasise the perception of the general workforce that work can produce a set of symptoms (which are well defined elsewhere in this book) to which is attached the diagnosis of stress. Lazarus defined stress as 'occurring when there are demands on the person which tax or exceed his adjustive resources' (Lazarus, 1976). This emphasises the individual nature of stress. Certain factors in the workplace are known to cause stress (Table 6.4). Workshops for defined work groups should facilitate the recognition of stress-inducing factors specific to their own work setting and should enable participants to address these issues in a constructive way. Apart from identifying stress symptoms in themselves it is also important for managers to be able to recognise problems in their staff and to have the skills to deal with the issues.

The thrust of such workshops is towards the individual, enabling each member of the workforce to identify signs and symptoms of stress in themselves, to identify causes of stress

Table 6.4 *Factors in workplace causing stress*

Unsatisfactory Working Conditions
Overload
Role Ambiguity
Role Conflict
Responsibility for People
Unsatisfactory Relationships
Under- or Overpromotion
Unhealthy Organisational Structure/Culture

in the workplace and to learn stress reduction techniques such as meditation and relaxation.

A programme of workshops will form part of the plan. As with lifeskills training, attendance at such workshops is voluntary but a significant percentage of personnel can be reached if workshops are available over a period of time when colleagues will encourage each other to attend.

Training to manage change. No one likes change. The poem below written by Machiavelli in the sixteenth century expresses this very well:

> No task is so difficult
> To set about
> No leadership so delicate
> No venture so hazardous
> As the attempt to introduce
> A new order of things
>
> Those who change
> Find as their adversaries
> All those who succeeded well
> Under the old order
> And no more than lukewarm
> Supporters among those who
> Might function under the new

If major change is envisaged in the workplace, the plan should include a strategy to minimise the adverse effects on staff. A successful and trouble-free change process depends on a number of factors (Table 6.5). Managers need to know how to manage change; how to change 'no' to 'yes'. Too often major change finds managers beleaguered with no skills or time resources to negotiate the change period successfully.

Table 6.5 *Managing successful change*

Workforce Involvement
Adequate Funding
General Security
Good Communications
Adequate Staff Support
Imaginative Redeployment
Good Redundancy Packages
Appropriate Time Scale

Where appropriate the plan will contain:

- A training programme for managers on managing
- A training programme for staff on coping with change
- A resettlement counselling scheme

Improving the Organisational Style

No amount of effort focused on the individual will increase well-being if the organisational style is destructive. It is not appropriate to this chapter to discuss at any length what constitutes a healthy management style. There are many organisations which retain the 'stick and carrot' method of management, where fear of censure or of job loss gives short-term productivity; and other organisations where management appears to be arbitrary, unfair or remote. In developing a health plan one cannot make the assumption that support for it indicates a healthy management style. The health plan may be seen as a method of papering the cracks.

Questionnaires such as the Occupational Stress Indicator (OSI) may highlight organisational problems. It is based on Cooper's definition of stress which enlarges the Lazarus definition (Cooper, Sloan & Williams, 1988) as 'a negatively perceived quality which as a result of inadequate coping with sources of stress has negative mental and physical ill health consequences'. As well as identifying sources of pressure for the individual it also identifies organisational dysfunction as seen by the individual. Analysis of the responses from groups of individuals in the same workplace can provide a powerful indicator of where the organisational problems lie.

Where serious cultural or organisational problems are identified during the assessment, the plan should include arrangements for the involvement of an organisational psychologist.

Development of Health-related policies

A number of personnel policies need to be developed to underpin the organisation's positive approach to mental health.

Sickness Absence

Inevitably in any organisation some people will become mentally ill. The nature of this illness will range from short-duration stress disorders to long-term psychotic illness. The organisation's Sickness Absence Policy should include guidance to managers on managing both long- and short-term absences. It should also encompass its position on rehabilitation and resettlement. Re-entry to the workplace of individuals who have suffered mental illness may provoke either considerable resistance on the part of colleagues or overprotectiveness.

Alcohol Misuse

There have been many attempts to quantify the extent of alcohol misuse in the workplace. Many organisations have developed sympathetic policies for the management of individuals with this problem. Unfortunately most cases remain concealed and form a small but disruptive element in many workforces. A well-developed and advertised alcohol policy should enable more successful management. Features of an alcohol policy are shown in Table 6.6. Management of drug dependency should be treated in a similar way but the legal implications do not allow for second chances. The plan should identify policies which need to be developed and provide guidelines for development.

Development of Staff Support Systems

Counselling

Counselling at an early stage can and does reduce poor performance and sickness absence (Reddy, 1992). The level of counselling provision will depend very much on the organisation. The original assessment should have given some indication on the level of need. In many instances there may be sufficient expertise within the human resource management and the occupational health teams.

Table 6.6 *Alcohol policy*

Restriction of Availability
Management Training
Health Education
Clear Personnel Procedures
Job Security

Where the need is great, consideration should be given to the recruitment of counsellors or to setting up a counselling provision externally using one of the many organisations providing such services. A full Employee Assistance Programme provides counselling for staff on many issues unrelated to work. Payment is usually on a per capita basis. Its cost may not be justified for average need when there is a reasonable level of expertise in-house.

Support Groups

For work groups where the pressure on staff is known to be great, such as health care workers, setting up local support groups may serve to protect employees' health and provide a useful method of defusing developing problems. These groups may provide useful indicators to organisational problems. To be effective such groups should be well constructed and their purpose must be clear. If not properly established they serve little useful purpose. The plan should contain recommendations on the provision of staff support.

Summary Plan

The plan should include:

1 An introduction including information on the possible effects of mental illness in performance and attendance.
2 The Health Safety and Welfare Policy statement.
3 A description of the organisation's structure and mores with reference to mental health.
4 Recommendations on recruitment procedures.

5   Recommendations   on   sickness   absence/resettlement procedures.
6   Draft policies on health-related topics such as:

sickness absence;
alcohol abuse;
smoking policies.

7   Training programmes for:

stress management;
change management;
lifeskills topics.

8   A management training programme.
9   Training packages and plans for all posts.
10   Proposals for an audit of:

organisational health including communications;
individual health.

11   Proposal for improved sickness absence analysis.
12   Proposals for any change in the provision of:

training;
occupational health;
counselling.

13   Proposals for organisational changes—although these would be expanded in another forum.
14   Estimated cost of each of these proposals.
15   A timetable for implementation.

IMPLEMENTATION

The Working Party will now have before them an assessment of the organisation's needs and a draft plan containing some of the elements described above, which they believe to be appropriate and for which resources are likely to be available in both the short and longer term.

This plan should now be referred to senior management and put out for consultation within the organisation. It is important not to raise false hopes or fears at this stage. Following consultations, a fully funded strategy for promoting and maintaining the mental health of the workforce should emerge.

Audit

Two forms of audit should be put in place at this time.

1 Audit of the effects of the plan on staff well-being and hence on performance. This may include:

 (a) comparison of OSI results in particular groups before implementation and one year later;
 (b) sickness absence statistics;
 (c) early retirement statistics;
 (d) staff turnover;
 (e) productivity (where appropriate);
 (f) measurement of lifestyle changes.

The benefits of this sort of initiative are not always easy to demonstrate and certainly the effects of lifestyle changes may take many years to show. If early assessment of the outcome is required it may be also appropriate to introduce a questionnaire looking at staff attitudes, morale and job satisfaction so that early trends can be identified.

2 Audit of the implementation of the plan. A date should be set, realistically around twelve months, to audit progress towards full implementation.

CONCLUSION

The opportunity to develop a Mental Health Plan should indicate a commitment at senior management level to the health of staff. If this commitment is to be sustained structures should be in place to measure expected outcomes. Too often occupational mental health initiatives are seen as an act of faith by a 'benevolent management'.

REFERENCES

Banham, J. (1992). The cost of mental ill health to business. In *Prevention of Mental Ill Health at Work*. London: HMSO.

Bertera, R. L. (1990). The effects of workplace health promotion on absenteeism and employment costs in a large industrial population. *American Journal of Public Health*, **80**, 9, 1101–1105.

Cooper, C. L., Sloan, S. & Williams, S. (1988). *Occupational Stress Indicator*. Windsor: NFER.

Cox, T. & Kuk, G. (1992). Healthiness of schools as organisations: Teacher stress and health. *Proceedings of International Congress on Stress, Anxiety and Emotional Disorders*, University of Minho, Portugal.

HMSO (1974). The Health and Safety at Work Act. London: HMSO.

HMSO (1992). The Health of the Nation. London: HMSO.

HMSO (1992). The Management of Health and Safety at Work Regulations—HSE. London: HMSO.

Jones, R. C., Bly, J. L. & Richardson, J. E. (1990). A study of a worksite health promotion programme and absenteeism. *Journal of Occupational Health*, **32**, 2, 95–99.

Lazarus, R. S. (1976). *Patterns of Adjustment*. New York: McGraw-Hill.

Reddy, M. (1992). Counselling, its Value to Business. *Prevention of Mental Ill Health at Work*. London: HMSO.

7
An Organisational Stress Audit: BNR Europe

CHRIS M. JUDGE
Human Resources Manager, Northern Telecom,
Canada

INTRODUCTION

Bell Northern Research is an internationally based research and development subsidiary of Northern Telecom, the world's leading supplier of fully digital telecommunications switching equipment. Northern Telecom has 60 000 staff and 48 manufacturing sites around the world, while BNR employs over 10 000 people in addition to this and has a global R & D presence which includes several major locations in the UK. Annually, BNR's R & D programmes represent an investment well in excess of $960 million. Northern Telecom's clients range from governments to major international organisations. Their products include switching and transmission systems, fibre optics, subscriber switching systems and telephones.

It is fair to say that the focus of the organisation is increasingly on the quality of its products (in this particular case, software). It can also be argued that a sustained high quality culture in an R & D environment can only be achieved through its people. Simply stating that 'Our People are Our

Creating Healthy Work Organizations. Edited by C. L. Cooper and S. Williams.
© 1994 John Wiley & Sons Ltd

Strength' on a set of company values is not enough and BNR has started to promote a quality culture amongst its staff. The stress audit and subsequent follow-up actions are indications of this.

The BNR lab in the UK, where the stress audit was commissioned, is in Maidenhead and is responsible for Switching Software Development for the European Market. It was set up in 1984 with a small group of engineers and rapidly grew to its current level of 350+ employees. In 1991, following the acquisition of STC, the numbers in BNR Europe grew to 1300 with employees now based at two other major sites in the UK. The structure of the lab is relatively flat with only five grades separating graduate entrants and the managing director. Of these, there are three engineering grades who all report directly into the first-level managers.

In view of the fact that the world market for telecommunications equipment and services is due to treble (by most estimations) to be worth around $300 billion by the year 2000, BNR's role is to work closely with Northern Telecom to supply workable solutions for these opportunities.

BACKGROUND TO THE INTRODUCTION OF THE SURVEY

Before going into detail as to why BNR chose to carry out a stress audit, it is important to understand the wider environment that the company was operating in. BNR took the view that stress at work is inescapable. However, in light of the factors listed below, the company wanted to know more about whether or not stress was having a detrimental effect on the staff.

First of all, following the economic boom years of the late 1980s, BNR's lab in Maidenhead had grown rapidly and 50% of the workforce were recruited in the period 1990–1991. This was partly as a result of expansion. However, the fact that the company was based in the Thames Valley area with considerable external opportunities meant that competition to recruit employees was strong and turnover of staff was relatively high. BNR believe that the reason why individuals were leaving to go to other companies was not because of stress or pressure but simply because they felt the need for a change after two to three years in the same job. The significant number of 'return employees' is an indication of this. However, the effect of that staff movement combined with the expansion of the workforce inevitably created its own pressure.

The second point is that the workforce, including the management team, was relatively young and inexperienced. On the plus side, the level of energy, commitment and enthusiasm was second to none! However, sometimes the calming influence of a few 'older heads' may have been missing. This, in fact, has been a major focus of attention following the stress audit. As with many engineering environments, the emphasis had been on technical excellence rather than managerial competence.

The third significant factor is the fact that the company was committed to an ambitious and aggressive schedule of customer deadlines which inevitably put increased demands on a young workforce, and particularly affected the managers.

Finally, the work itself involved constantly changing and evolving technology, organisation structures and customer requirements. Whilst employees had to learn to live with this change, when combined with other factors it may have caused increased pressure. A need was therefore created to know and understand more about the effects of stress on the workforce and what, if anything, the company should do about it.

Another reason for looking into stress concerned the desire to benchmark against other organisations. One noteworthy fact about companies in the latter half of the twentieth century is the amount of time and money that is spent on ensuring the competitiveness of the package they offer to employees. BNR was no different and, as a company, we felt that we had got the pay and benefits right. Constant surveys were entered into to ensure our salaries were competitive and the benefits were generous. They included a very wide-ranging car policy for managers, private health and dental cover for all employees, and a very beneficial savings scheme. The work surroundings were excellent. Employees worked in modern air-conditioned offices with spacious work stations, and so on. However, in common with most companies, BNR had no reliable data on the environment it provided for its employees or whether the culture of the organisation was supportive and, as a result, was keen to benchmark itself against other leading companies in terms of the levels of stress and pressure.

Recognising the importance of following up the survey, we also needed to identify any particular areas or groups where the levels of stress might be higher and to take appropriate action. At this stage we had no clear idea as to what would be found or indeed what remedial action would be required.

Preparation

Having established contact with an external stress audit consultancy, what we needed first was to identify areas into which employees would fit neatly for the purpose of analysis. Five groups of employees (e.g. designers, planners, etc.) were chosen plus a sixth 'other' category to accommodate the rest. There were also categories for three levels of employee—non-management, first-level management and senior management —as well as for the gender of those taking part and their length of service. In a relatively flat organisation structure this seemed to work well, although it is worth noting that with follow-up surveys these groupings will have to be fine-tuned to reflect current organisation structures.

A number of structured discussion groups were then arranged so that a representative from the consultancy could get a better feel for the 'culture' of the lab. The discussion groups were designed to add some qualitative data to the quantitative statistics that the audit would produce. Last of all, agreement had to be reached on the timing and communication of the audit. When would the workforce first be told about the stress audit and why we wanted to carry it out? How could BNR make it as easy as possible to complete the questionnaire, using either a paper copy or a computer disk version? What was the minimum percentage needed to be returned? We would have liked an 80% return rate within two months and actually achieved 70% in nearly three months. One reason for this was the fact that the questionnaires were handed out in

June and July at the start of the holiday season. A second significant reason was that as the company is committed to quality and excellence, it is constantly reviewing its progress with employees. There is therefore a slight danger of survey 'overkill'. For example all employees had recently been invited to take part in a separate corporate satisfaction survey.

RESULTS

The results of the survey can be summarised as follows:

1 Compared with the general population the employees of the BNR Europe Maidenhead lab did not report significantly higher levels of mental and physical ill health nor did they report lower levels of job satisfaction. These scales of the Occupational Stress Indicator (OSI) summarise the effects of stress on an individual and the data suggest that the 'average' employee within BNR perceived the effects of the stress process in a similar way to the average employee in other organisations in both the public and the private sectors. In short it means that stress is no more and no less of a problem for BNR than for many other organisations (see Figure 7.1).

2 The BNR employees reported similar levels of pressure to employees in other organisations. They perceived more than average pressure from the home–work interface, career and achievement, and the job itself but less pressure from their managerial role and the organisational forces. The BNR employees had similar scores to employees in similar companies on the scales measuring Type A behaviour but felt that they had much more control and influence over their managerial role and their individual ability to make things happen. They did not appear to make as much use of coping mechanisms as employees in other organisations and, although the differences were not massive, the BNR group did not appear to be coping as well as they might. This was particularly true in the use of logic, time management and the home–work interface.

120

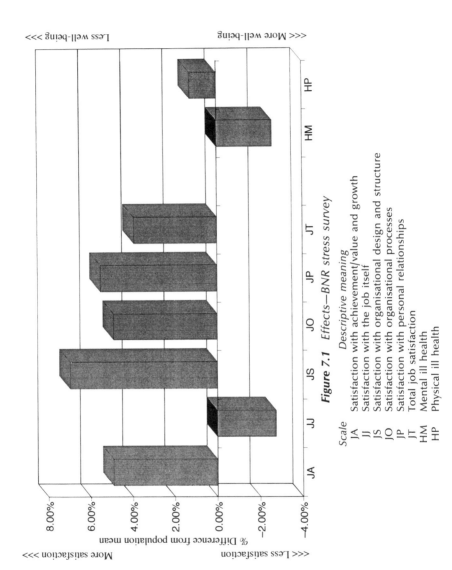

Figure 7.1 Effects—BNR stress survey

Scale   Descriptive meaning
JA   Satisfaction with achievement/value and growth
JJ   Satisfaction with the job itself
JS   Satisfaction with organisational design and structure
JO   Satisfaction with organisational processes
JP   Satisfaction with personal relationships
JT   Total job satisfaction
HM   Mental ill health
HP   Physical ill health

3 The managerial group at Maidenhead appeared to suffer more from occupational stress than their counterparts in other industries. The most striking feature of the analysis was the low level of control and influence over the organisational processes. Most managers in other industries perceived themselves as having the ability to control the way the organisation worked and the more senior the managers the more autonomy they had. In BNR managers compared unfavourably with their peers elsewhere.

4 The effects of stress were not uniformly distributed but affected some areas more than others. The internal comparisons highlighted the areas with the highest and lowest job satisfaction levels. Women reported less job satisfaction than the men and job satisfaction seemed to be at its lowest for those employees who had been in their jobs for more than one and less than three years (see Figure 7.2).

5 The total Type A behaviour scores show that women tended to have lower Type A behaviour than men and that the most extreme Type A behaviours were to be found in the senior managers. These results were typical for most companies; however, what was interesting was that those people who had been in their job for less than 12 months demonstrated higher Type A behaviour than those who had been in their jobs for longer.

6 The pressure from the job itself seemed to affect women more than men and again the report highlighted the department where pressure was greatest. Pressure from the job seemed to affect first-level managers more than their colleagues at other levels and did not seem to be a problem for those employees who had been in their job for more than three years.

7 Communication seemed to be a problem within the Maidenhead lab. Poor communications, although not directly measured by the OSI, underlay many of the negative effects of the stress process. The focus groups made particular mention of communication problems and felt that this was an issue for upward, downward and sideways communication. It appeared that communication and involvement were good where product or operational issues were concerned but fell down in other areas, especially 'people' issues.

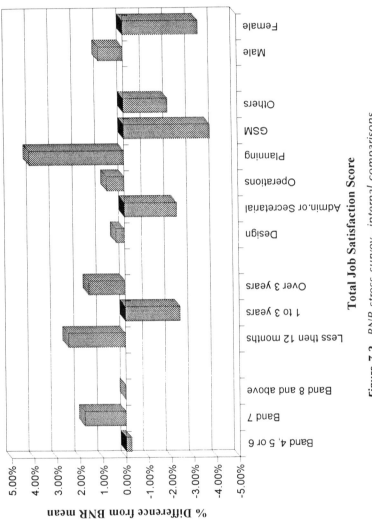

Figure 7.2 *BNR stress survey—internal comparisons*

8 Goal setting appeared to be a source of pressure to the managers and employees in the Maidenhead lab. There was a feeling that goals were set without enough involvement from the people who had to achieve the results. This tendency to overcommit might leave employees without a sense of success and completion if the targets were unrealistic.

These results, whilst by no means perfect, were encouraging for two main reasons. The first is that the stress audit indicated the overall levels of pressure were no higher on average than in other similar industries or for that matter throughout industry in general. The effects of stress reported by the BNR Maidenhead staff were similar to those reported by employees in other companies.

The second reason is that the results highlighted the fact that the ability to 'cope' with stress was consistently lower at all levels. This result is encouraging because, to a large extent, coping skills can be taught. This can be illustrated by looking at the '4-Way Model' illustrated in Figure 7.3. The model shows that an increase in the sources of pressure produces a corresponding increase in the negative effects. An improvement in the coping mechanisms counterbalances the effects of pressure and a change in personality will influence the degree

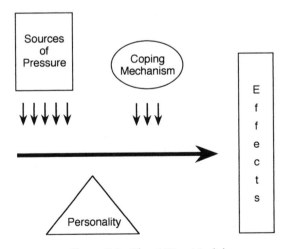

Figure 7.3 *The 4-Way Model*

to which a given source of pressure will produce a negative or positive outcome.

What this meant in real terms is that BNR could introduce some practical measures to help their employees cope more effectively with stress. That is not to say they were not coping adequately, it was simply that their coping mechanisms were not as refined as those of employees in other companies. As a result the company was able to introduce a series of training initiatives to help address the skills shortages, including time management and stress management training.

At this stage it is probably appropriate to focus on the detailed report itself and go through the major recommendations in order to highlight the actions that BNR has been able to take.

RECOMMENDATIONS

The first recommendation concentrated on improving the ability to cope with pressure. It recommended developing a programme to raise the awareness and use of a broad range of coping mechanisms. In particular, BNR made more visible and accessible the existing range of time management and stress management programmes and increased their frequency where appropriate. Project management training was also, and continues to be, a focus of attention.

The second recommendation looked at the relative lack of control and influence that the managers felt they had. This has been explored in more detail and a number of actions spread over the next three years are now being worked through. First of all, there has been a shift in emphasis away from technical training and on to management development. The average number of days spent attending such programmes has risen dramatically. This has also coincided with the growth of corporate-driven leadership training programmes that focus on the company's core values. Amongst other things attention is devoted to the personal development of newly promoted managers, although this is recognised as an on-going long-term process.

In addition, specific individual training and development is being targeted through the use of a 4-way feedback exercise, an upwards appraisal report which is based on a series of management competencies. The 4-way feedback analyses responses from direct reports, peers and senior managers of how well a manager performs against those competencies and is used entirely as a development tool. The individual managers themselves also complete the questionnaire. The real advantage is not so much that they can compare themselves against a BNR norm but that they can focus on very specific areas for development. This can then be addressed with specific training and development rather than adopting a broad brush management skills course approach. All managers and directors in the Maidenhead laboratory will have been through this process by the end of 1993.

Significantly, all potential candidates for promotion (into a management position) are also now obliged to attend a management development centre which assesses their suitability to manage people. Again this is a development exercise. It is not for approving or turning down promotions but it puts forward recommendations, based on the observations of two days of exercises and tests. The feedback is given verbally back in the work location by one of the assessors and is given to the individual and his or her manager together.

The third recommendation suggested paying particular attention to the department that showed the lowest job satisfaction level. The fact that it showed a lower job satisfaction level came as something of a surprise as it was arguably the most successful self-contained group on site. However, on closer analysis, there were some good reasons. First of all, the timing of the audit coincided with a particularly critical time, in terms of the deliverables, of the group and individuals were under pressure at work. Secondly, the group, which had been set up from scratch only one year earlier, had experienced some considerable churn in its programme content which to an extent brought frustration to the group. Finally, as a result of reorganisation, there was a change in the senior management team and in the reporting structure which in turn brought uncertainty.

Having accepted that the results could be rationalised, BNR was still keen to address the issue. The senior manager concerned brought up the subject at his regular weekly meeting to the whole group. He invited feedback and a very frank discussion took place as to why this was the case and how it could be turned around. What evolved from this and subsequent discussions with his managers was a desire for an off-site team-building session for the whole group. This eventually took place in late November 1992 and was combined with the successful completion of the next phase of the project.

The fourth recommendation talked of introducing programmes that might enhance the role of women at work. This was because the pressure from the job seemed to affect women more than men. Exactly why this was the case is still unsure although the consultants have been asked to do some further analysis to help better understanding of the issue.

Another recommendation stated that goal setting should, if possible, be made more realistic and ideally more 'participative'. As a result, a series of training programmes have been introduced explaining the company's appraisal system. These are designed for employees to get the most out of their appraisals and, in particular, to help them feel more involved when goals are set.

As well as this, all managers are required to undergo training both in appraisal interviewing and in objective setting prior to conducting staff appraisals. In order to measure success and progress, a People Performance Management Assessment survey is carried out quarterly across NT and BNR sites. This asks a random set of employees about such matters as whether their objectives have been discussed and approved in a timely manner, and the results can be broken down on a division basis.

The final recommendation addressed the issue of communications throughout the BNR Maidenhead lab. This is an issue that has been a focus of attention for some time across BNR and NT. There are now some very sophisticated tools to help the communication process, ranging from the latest video conference technology through to increasingly refined computer network and electronic mail capabilities. In addition, a corporate reports video is produced quarterly and sent to all senior managers with the intention of their cascading that information down to their staff. However, it is still communication at a local level that needs enhancing both upwards and downwards. Individuals felt that they needed to be given more positive unsolicited feedback. The report also recommended using more team-building events which enable employees to have their views listened to.

In order to address this, several things have happened which may not be new but have been given increased focus and attention. The first concerns the area of positive feedback. Whilst there is no substitute for a timely and genuine 'Thank you' or 'Congratulations', managers are being encouraged also to take advantage of the Recognition Awards Scheme (where individual employees or teams can be financially rewarded for their contribution).

In terms of team events, these have been adopted in a number of areas and broadly can be split into two types: those of a celebratory nature, such as when the lab was formally given ISO 9001 accreditation; and those with a more specific communication purpose, such as the bi-monthly General Information Session to all employees. This is presented by the managing director, who invites in guest 'speakers' as appropriate. Additionally, the senior management team on site together attended a Process of Management Visionary Workshop. Since then, a number of that team have taken away their own managers and senior members of staff to help build a shared vision for their department and then, most importantly, communicate it to all employees.

BENEFITS

As with many such initiatives, the specific benefits are hard to quantify, particularly over the short term. Are the levels of pressure lower and has the ability to cope with stress improved? Has morale increased and is there now a greater level of job satisfaction? Most of these questions are difficult to answer since they require subjective judgements and, even if the results are clear, they are usually only visible over a longer period of time. It could be argued that having a lower turnover of staff is an indication of success. However, if that coincides with a period of very high unemployment and deep recession, as happened with BNR, then such low attrition is expected. Similarly, as the country begins to show the signs of economic recovery, labour turnover is likely to increase, particularly with such a young, mobile workforce. Is this an indication of failure?

Perhaps the most difficult or frustrating aspect of this study is making an attempt to link any improvement directly to the changes that were made as a result of the survey. Would they not have happened anyway as the senior management team evolved? In the opinion of the HR group there is a link but it will take longer for it to become visible. The stress audit seems to have helped the workforce, and, in particular, the management team, to become more aware of the factors that cause stress but the full benefits may not be seen for several years yet. In the short to medium term, however, it has helped to improve targeting of training and development initiatives, particularly at a management level.

By involving all members of the workforce, the stress audit has arguably helped to increase morale. Everybody likes to feel that they have a say in the running of their company, or at least a contribution to make to it, and commenting on issues that affect the levels of satisfaction is an important factor. Northern Telecom and BNR have published commitments to raise not only the level of customer satisfaction but also the level of employee satisfaction to 95% + by 1997, and to demonstrate their commitment to this, senior managers will be rewarded (through their annual bonus) if they meet and exceed such targets.

There is, of course, an important pitfall to avoid here and that is ensuring that the stress audit is not regarded as yet another staff or attitude survey. As has already been illustrated, follow-up actions must take place. Furthermore, not only must they take place but they must be seen to have taken place. Specific communication to all employees pointing out what is happening and what will happen as a result is vital. Also important, as BNR noted with the follow-up audit, is reminding employees what did happen, as such initiatives are not always visible to everyone.

A further benefit is the increased awareness and understanding of stress amongst employees and how they can deal with it. Whilst it is commonplace to talk openly and constructively about stress in many North American based companies (including BNR and NT) it still seems to be something of a taboo subject in the UK, although this situation appears to be improving. Such an awareness of stress and its positive and negative effects may be increasing, however there still seems to be a prevailing view or assumption that stress is negative and that it happens 'elsewhere'. It is just 'not the done thing' to talk about the stress of your colleagues other than in concerned whispers, verging on gossip! The company believes that the initial audit and its subsequent follow-up will help break this taboo. Stress, in both its positive and negative effects, should be discussed in an open and constructive manner.

The final benefit concerns the area of measurability. Whilst acknowledging the fact that it is very difficult to quantify levels of satisfaction and morale, by committing to a follow-up audit the company will at least have a measure of how it is 'progressing' (rather than relying on subjective judgements). This is important for a number of reasons. First of all, morale is a bit like the economy after a long recession, in that it can be talked up or down. If morale is poor and people complain about it, it gets worse (or at least, gets no better). However, if it is improving, even by small amounts, then it has a beneficial effect (once again, the importance of follow-up action is demonstrated here).

A second reason that it is important to be able to measure progress is because of the inevitability of change within the senior management team. Whilst the current members may remember what it was like in 1991–1992, there is every chance that in three to four years time the majority of these decision-makers will have moved on to different jobs as their careers progress. It will be necessary, therefore, to have something that future managers can use as a reference, particularly if it helps to avoid errors made in the past and to ensure continuity.

ENSURING SUCCESS

As already stressed, the importance of getting the communication right should not be underestimated. Employees must be informed about what is happening and when it is happening, and they should be kept involved. The idea for the initial stress audit came from one of the directors and the Human Resources/Occupational Health Department and was in response to some specific individual concerns at BNR. However, all follow-up action, including the next audit has been done in consultation with employees. The site at Maidenhead is a non-unionised environment and consultation here has been through the lab council, an informal staff association, and the managers.

Once the results have been published, full access should be given to all employees. Edited or summarised versions may create suspicion or mistrust if the original is not made available. In fact, BNR did three things to communicate the findings:

1   Managers were invited to a presentation of the results given by the consultancy. A copy of the slides used, summarising the results, was made available for them to cascade that information. This was an opportunity for them to question the findings and gain a better understanding.
2   All employees were contacted directly, via electronic mail, with a further summary of the findings.
3   In addition to the above communication, employees were also informed that the original report would be kept in the Information Resource Centre on site and could be viewed at any time.

Following publication the most important communication then follows, that is, what happens next or as a result. Cynics in any workforce may well argue that in the rapidly changing 1990s, stress audits are just the latest 'flavour of the month' initiative. Asking people about their levels of stress and pressure does not in itself relieve such pressure unless it is followed up with positive action and a longer term commitment to further audits. Ensuring that people are aware of the on-going action through regular communication helps to demonstrate this commitment.

At BNR there has been follow-up communication, initially about three months after the results were first published and then again six months later in anticipation of the second audit. With the benefit of hindsight, it might be argued that more communication could have happened with perhaps regular updates. Certainly, as it is the first time that such an initiative has been conducted in the UK, it is better to overcommunicate than to assume employees are informed.

Another pitfall to avoid is that the stress audit might be regarded as just a personnel department initiative. Fortunately at BNR the senior management team not only supported this initiative, they actively sponsored its introduction and are committed to a follow-up. Whilst the majority of personnel and human resources departments in this country may have shaken off the 'caring welfare' image, it is still important on exercises such as this to get the buy-in of managers and thereby ensure that it gets real attention and is viewed with importance and credibility. If there is not this buy-in from the top then the chances of getting enough meaningful data back must be reduced.

For those companies considering conducting a stress survey for the first time, there are some learning points from the exercise. BNR had a relatively young workforce which in itself may have contributed to the pressure and stress but such a workforce was also arguably more receptive to, or less suspicious of, the idea of a stress survey. A different company with an older age profile amongst the employees might need to think carefully about how the message is communicated. As already stated, BNR also made a commitment to carry out follow-up surveys, thus ensuring that it was viewed not as a reactionary measure but as part of a long-term plan.

The benefits to BNR will become visible over a longer period of time as long as recommendations continue to be acted upon. However, conducting the stress audit should not simply be regarded as a solution in its own right but should be viewed as part of a long-term plan for improving the work environment and maximising productivity. It should also help to improve the levels of employee satisfaction as they feel confident that they have a say and that their comments are acted upon. There is a long way to go yet and getting the communication right is the key to it all, and a positive step in the right direction.

CONCLUSION

BNR is a relatively young company in the UK in a rapidly changing and evolving industry. Because of concern amongst some of the senior management team and human resources department a need to find out more about the levels of stress was created. As a result the company was put in touch with the consultancy and the Occupational Stress Indicator. The OSI not only helped to quantify perceived levels of stress and pressure but allowed comparisons to be made against other companies. It also gave useful indications on measures such as job satisfaction amongst a wide cross-section of groups within the company so that follow-up action could be specifically targeted.

The report itself was written in sufficient detail to cover a wide range of topics and yet was also written in a language that could be clearly understood by all. The actual results generated gave BNR a good deal of information. Some of it came as a surprise but other results confirmed existing beliefs and in some cases concerns. The report has given BNR the chance to take a long-term view on a wide range of issues that affect its workforce.

Overall the process seemed to have been viewed positively by those who took part at BNR but the momentum generated through the recommendations should not be lost. Expectations have been raised and must now be met. However, just as important is the information the audit has provided and should continue to provide towards future development initiatives. In conjunction with other more traditional sources of information, it should enable the company to put forward realistic, attainable development plans and to periodically check the progress of those plans in years to come.

8
Managing Stress at Work: The ICI–Zeneca Pharmaceuticals Experience 1986–1993

ERIC L. TEASDALE
Chief Medical Officer, Zeneca Pharmaceuticals
STEVE MCKEOWN
Consultant Psychiatrist, and UK President of the
International Stress Management Association

HEALTH AND STRESS

Health has been defined in many ways. Amongst them are:

a state of complete physical, mental and social well-being, not merely the absence of disease or infirmity.

. . . a personal experience of positive enjoyment of life.

In the occupational or industrial setting, the emphasis on maintaining *mental* (as well as physical and social) well-being is essential to success. Occasional serious cases of mental illness must be recognised and managed appropriately. This should

Creating Healthy Work Organizations. Edited by C. L. Cooper and S. Williams.
© 1994 John Wiley & Sons Ltd

include the care of the individual who has a problem of substance abuse (e.g. alcohol or drugs of addiction), and the patient with a psychotic condition where prompt admission to hospital is required. In practice, however, the more common mental health problems encompass stress, anxiety and depression, and their manifestation in the workplace.

The authors attended a workshop on stress which took place in Manchester in 1985. Both had been interested in stress-related psychiatric illness for some time and had concluded that there was a fundamental problem in the delivery of mental health care in England, which has arisen largely as a result of historical accident. Skills, experience and resources have been concentrated in acute psychiatric hospitals where teams of specialised staff essentially wait for patients to become sufficiently ill to be referred for treatment. Psychiatric care is still stigmatised in England, and the need for psychiatric referral in itself produces stress. The threshold for referral into such care is unrealistically high. Illnesses become unnecessarily severe and patients often wait an unreasonably long time before receiving help. For clinical, humane and economic reasons, it would seem appropriate in an enlightened society to embark on preventive psychiatry and to aim to detect and treat disturbance at an earlier stage.

We listened to a variety of presentations ranging from the academic to the philosophical, but all obsessed with the definition of stress and the sociological and political issues related to its causation. Suggestions and models for stress management presented were idiosyncratic, fragmented and reflected more the preoccupations of the various stress management consultants, rather than any planned or comprehensive approach. As a result of this we agreed to try to assess the problem within ICI Pharmaceuticals and to develop suitable responses.

The motivation for action in ICI Pharmaceuticals resulted from a steadily increasing referral load of known stress-related illness. It was understood that many employees conceal their stress-related illness from their managers, fearing that they may be seen as weak or as poor prospects for promotion and increased responsibility. These attitudes were thought to persist despite evidence to the contrary, and as a result the number of cases known to any company will only ever be the tip of an iceberg of unknown size. ICI Pharmaceuticals, as a sophisticated and caring employer, was committed to the development of a comprehensive service for mental as well as physical health.

Background

On 1 January 1993, ICI's Pharmaceuticals business together with the Agrochemicals and Seeds and Specialties Business became the constituent members of Zeneca Limited. On 1 June 1993 Zeneca was demerged from ICI and became a separate public limited company. 'New' ICI now consists of the remaining international businesses, namely Paints, Industrial Chemicals, Materials, Explosives and Tioxide Ltd.

Zeneca Pharmaceuticals is a large organisation and the reader may benefit from hearing something of the dimensions, characteristics and 'mission' statement of this business. This will allow the activities described to be put in context. In terms of *dimensions*, the business in 1992, had a turnover in excess of £1.6 billion sterling and sold its products in 130 countries. Manufacturing took place in 17 countries and 13 000 people were involved in the total operations. Research and development 'spend' amounted to £220 million per annum, which is approximately 14% of sales. Products which have recently been launched include 'Zestril' (a medicine for cardio-vascular conditions), 'Diprivan' (an anaesthetic) and 'Zoladex' (an anti-cancer agent). There is an exciting new product development pipeline which includes 'Merrem' (an antibiotic), 'Casodex' (an anti-cancer agent) and 'Accolate' (a novel therapy for asthma).

In terms of *geographical spread*, of the 13 000 employed in the business, 4400 work in the UK, 3500 in Continental Western Europe, 2800 in USA, 800 in Japan and 1500 in territories located in the rest of the world. By function, 4700 are involved in Sales and Marketing, 3600 in Manufacturing, 3300 in Research and Development and 1400 in Administration.

The pharmaceuticals industry is an extremely competitive sector in which to operate and is exposed to pressures which can translate themselves into high levels of stress in individuals. It is also largely research-orientated, depending on a high degree of creativity with long periods of uncertainty as to the final outcome of expensive development programmes. Such factors compound the pressure on individuals. Tight control of costs, a high volume of new work, the drive for high quality and compliance with Regulatory Authority requirements and the law all make the working environment tough and demanding.

It is essential for any organisation to define clearly the main areas of activity and thereby target resources appropriately. The 'Mission' of Zeneca Pharmaceuticals is 'To contribute to human health by providing worthwhile products which enable the business to grow and the people in it to prosper and lead fulfilling lives'. An enormous amount of work is going into the research and development of new medicines and the current objective is to bring one new product through to launch each year. To achieve this and to ensure that the established business thrives, it is essential to have a 'healthy' organisation. This implies having healthy people who are motivated and clearly focused on the job in hand. Ultimately the success of any business depends on the people in it.

Understanding and Quantifying the Problem

There was obvious concern about the casualty rate and general acceptance that the organisation was experiencing high stress levels which were damaging for many individuals. (Statistics are provided in the section on measurable benefits of Stress Management Workshops.) In common with most, if not all, Occupational Health Departments for large organisations, ICI received large amounts of unsolicited material relating to stress management and was also aware of the existence of Employee Assistance Programmes (EAPs). These commercially available stress management packages were in their infancy in the UK in 1986, and those available were clearly incomplete, overpriced or unethical—sometimes all three. A quotation from the novelist Alison Lurie is particularly relevant to many stress management initiatives: 'and their courses to be composed of equal parts of common sense and nonsense, that is, of the already obvious and the probably false'.

Why Not Buy an Employee Assistance Programme?

Employee Assistance Programmes have been an established part of the US employment culture for more than 20 years. In essence they provide confidential counselling which is usually on-site, funded by the employer, and conducted either by trained in-house staff or by external consultants. The EAP industry grew rapidly within the US, peaking in the mid 1980s. It was then a predictable and well-researched activity which claimed to have demonstrated good cost benefits at an American take-up rate of approximately six employees per thousand per annum. The industry developed haphazardly in the UK, originally by the transplantation into Europe of EAPs which had been home grown by American parent organisations. It is noteworthy that EAPs originally grew out of alcoholism treatment in the US; the identification and management of addictions is still a major focus.

Early UK experience suggested that EAPs were perceived differently by UK employees who take up the service more readily, but often with social, domestic or financial problems rather than addictions or psychological distress. Traditionally UK employers have not needed to involve themselves actively in the health care of their employees, leaving such provision to the National Health Service and latterly in combination with private health care funded by private health insurance schemes. Every UK resident is entitled to the services of an NHS family doctor without payment for a service and the traditional EAP model does not sit comfortably alongside existing services. For these and other reasons, ICI Pharmaceuticals, in common with most major UK employers, had chosen not to follow the EAP model.

Internal Research

In 1986, 656 employees working in another ICI business of similar size and profile were sent copies of the 12-item General Health Questionnaire (GHQ-12, Goldberg, 1972) through the internal mail and invited to complete and return them in confidence. A total of 81% were returned, of which 77% were usable. 'Caseness', that is positive evidence of psychiatric morbidity, was detected in 19%: the typical sufferer was male, aged 40–49 and in a managerial or administrative job. This detection rate was higher than many other sample populations.

We have already explained why the pharmaceuticals industry is an extremely competitive sector in which to operate and much exposed to pressure—which can translate itself into high levels of stress on individuals. It is largely research-orientated, depending on a high degree of creativity with long periods of uncertainty as to the final outcome of expensive development programmes. Such factors compound the pressure on individuals. It is estimated that 1.5 million working days are lost in the UK each year through stress-related illness: any initiative to remedy this is to be welcomed. In addition to lost time, if employees are under excessive and prolonged pressures for too long, this can lead to an increased incidence of unsafe working practices and accidents in the workplace. There can also be a loss of 'creative edge' and poor performance and low morale may also result.

Most organisations provide no more than a casualty service, involving nurses and/or occupational physicians who recognise casualties and deal with them appropriately. It is, we believe, essential to have a positive strategy to manage stress, to make it a subject for legitimate discussion and to recognise stress-related conditions as having the potential for disrupting efficiency and productivity. Managing health is best recognised as part of the 'line management' responsibility. Managers should manage people as well as tasks, plant and projects. In order to achieve this, close liaison with the occupational health and personnel functions is likely to be required.

The ICI Pharmaceuticals culture dictated that problems are best handled when their extent has been quantified. Senior managers in any company would hold this view, that is that any problem can best be handled if it is possible to measure the extent of the situation or the number of people affected. In other words, *if you want to 'manage' then being able to 'measure' is essential*. Clearly, problems which relate to individual health need to be handled with sensitivity and confidentiality needs to be protected at all costs. There will be occasions when the manager is unaware of the difficulties being experienced by individuals, but senior management must understand the overall picture. Self-awareness and self-management must be promoted—the individual should be encouraged to learn skills and be aware of how he or she copes with increasing demands placed on them.

What is 'Stress'—a Working Model

A strategy was developed in order to promote a clear, simple message about stress and stress management within the organisation. This formed a subject of departmental briefings, hand-outs and leaflets and a trainers' manual written to accompany workshop material. Throughout the remainder of this chapter appropriate extracts from the manual will be included in italics.

One observer described 'stress' as 'a reality like love or electricity— unmistakable in experience but hard to define'. Stress is, of course, not confined to the workplace but may be related to home life and the social scene. 'OCCUPATIONAL STRESS' can mean either the pressure that work puts on individuals or the effect of that pressure. All work puts some pressure on individuals; in general the more demanding the work the greater the stress. This normally leads to higher output and satisfaction with work. However, a point of diminishing returns is reached beyond which increasing stress leads to reversed effects: lowered efficiency, job satisfaction, performance and mental well-being (Cooper & Marshall, 1980). **Stress itself is not an illness; rather it is a state. However it is a very powerful cause of illness. Long-term excessive stress is known to lead to serious health problems.**

Recent years have seen a bewildering array of books, magazine articles, television programmes and training courses about stress. Some of these can help you find out what stress is, but they rarely give you much of an idea what you can do about it. Stress is best thought of as a series of physical and mental reflexes which exist because they have had a purpose. They are designed to put your body and mind into overdrive for short periods of time, and to help your system to deal with short-term crises. It is presumably because they have a survival value that they have been bred into us in times long gone—the fastest runners and the hardest fighters were the ones who survived.

The problem for us in the modern world is that few of the pressures on us which produce stress, so called 'stressors', can be dealt with by direct physical action—no matter how much we might be tempted by the idea. The aim of quickly getting rid of the stress is usually hard to achieve. As a result we are left with the physical and mental effects of stress over periods of weeks, months or even years since the stressors that we have to deal with do not go away.

Many people feel that experiencing unpleasant stress is a weakness or that they should be able to use their mind or their logic to switch stress off. That is unrealistic; most of us have had the experience of feeling jittery after a 'near miss' in the car, even though we know that the threat has passed and we are completely safe. The stress responses are a set of automatic reflexes which are there to protect us and cannot be switched off.

Figure 8.1 depicts the relationship between stress, or pressure/demands on the individual (along the horizontal axis), and performance or output (the vertical axis)—this is sometimes called the 'Human Function Curve' and provides an important model in aiding understanding of the negative effects of stress.

This relationship can be demonstrated for physical responses to stress (e.g. the changes which can be observed in breathing rate and blood pressure) and psychological performance (e.g. performing mental arithmetic under time pressures), or in terms of group performance such as the productivity or efficiency of an organisation.

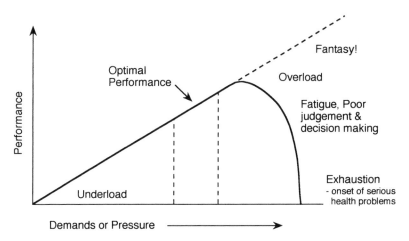

Figure 8.1 The relationship between stress and performance

Note that initially performance improves under pressure, this is why athletes often produce better results when competing than they do in practice sessions. The whole science of training and sports coaching is aimed at building competitors up to optimal performance for the day of the big event. However, this improvement does not go on forever. There comes a point where performance begins to deteriorate—an experience that all of us will have recognised in others, if not in ourselves. If the pressure is not reduced, then performance is sub-optimal and may even lead to breakdown.

We all perform at our best when under the right amount of pressure. There comes a point when the pressure becomes too much and our performance suffers. It is important to be aware of the consequences and notice when our efficiency is beginning to fall off. *Most people are unable to monitor their own stress levels but better at seeing it in colleagues or in friends or family. Brief overload does nothing more than temporarily reduce performance, major overload can prolong serious problems.* **Stress, of course, is a normal part of life. The challenge is to manage the pressures so that life is productive and enjoyable.**

In an organisation, or at the work place, the spectrum of effects ranges from minor inefficiency and lack of creativity to absenteeism, organisational breakdown, industrial relations problems or even sabotage (Table 8.1). In many organisations,

Table 8.1 The consequences of stress to a company/organisation

Reduced productivity
Increased errors
Lack of creativity
Poor decisions
Job dissatisfaction
Disloyalty
Increased sick leave
Unpreparedness
Premature retirement
Absenteeism
Accidents
Thefts
Organisational breakdown
Sabotage

Table 8.2   *The consequences of stress to the individual*

Anxiety
Fatigue
Insomnia
Boredom
Relationship problems
Emotional instability
Depression
Psychosomatic diseases
Health breakdowns (cardio-vascular)
Alcoholism
Drug abuse
Eating disorders
Suicide

only quite serious consequences in the bottom half of the list are monitored or recognised.

Negative effects in individuals can be manifest as fatigue, insomnia or inefficiency, through to more serious health problems such as heart disease, indigestion and peptic ulceration, excessive smoking, 'drinking', and anxiety or depression. (Table 8.2.)

THE ICI–ZENECA APPROACH

In the mid 1980s, the number of cases of stress-related illness in ICI Pharmaceuticals reported to the Occupational Health Department indicated a disturbing upward trend, as has already been noted. It may be of interest to display *three case histories* (identity is disguised but content is real) which demonstrate how stress-related problems can be manifested.

Mr A has to co-ordinate the submission of the information to obtain a product licence for a new compound. He works night and day—co-ordinating the efforts of people from individual departments. He has been told—'the business depends on you'. His free time shrinks, his wife and family get the rough edge of his tongue over many months, he feels unsupported at work and unable to say he can't cope. At 9 p.m. after a train journey from London he bursts into tears on the station platform. Six months later he still lacks confidence but is learning to work more effectively and still find time for himself and his family.

Mrs B is engaged in a number of negotiations with other companies. New projects and negotiations are initiated regularly and require concentration over long hours. The projects require managing—she plays a key role in supporting and advancing each one. Work starts at 8 a.m. and never seems to stop. Holidays and weekends don't exist. Hobbies are a thing of the past. She wishes manpower requirements to manage new projects were planned at the outset. On two occasions she has been seen leaving her office at 9 p.m. Eventually she is taken off her job for two weeks rest. Mrs B is lucky—her overwork was recognised as such and she is not considered to have failed. Others are branded as 'weak'.

Mr C is promoted to senior staff level. He is well trained and capable. He works hard but is unable to prioritise his tasks and give each one full attention. No one asks him to outline his workload and allocate appropriate time to each task. He works 10 or 11 hours daily and is usually busy with work at weekends. The initial enthusiasm at the promotion is replaced by anxiety. He feels desperate, panic-stricken and becomes depressed. One month's intensive treatment as an outpatient restores his health, vigour and enthusiasm. He needs training in managing his time. His manager needs not only to delegate the authority to look after various aspects of the departmental workload but also to share some of the responsibility for completion—within appropriate timescales.

Senior members of the occupational health and personnel functions met in late 1987 and a paper was drafted for presentation to the Chairman and Board of Directors of the business. Within that paper, the likely reasons for the increase in the number of stress cases within the Pharmaceuticals business were highlighted. The list is probably applicable to many other organisations:

- Rapid growth
- Increasing complexity
- Organisational change to meet growth
- Drive to become truly 'international'
- Pressure to sustain a high level of profit
- Pressure to bring new products to the market
- Tight control of manpower
- Sheer volume of new work
- High quality of work expected
- Commitment reaching a level where guilt is felt whenever work is not being done
- Difficulty in matching people to jobs
- The volume of paper

It was acknowledged that many of the people who get to the more senior jobs are relatively tough and resilient. For that reason, they may find it hard to understand why some of their subordinates find difficulty in coping. Stress may, however, affect individuals at all levels. The Board was asked, using the management system, to acknowledge the legitimacy of the concern and the proposals they were supporting to respond to it. The Board committed itself to a number of specific actions:

1   Staff should ensure that they deal with essential tasks and are selective in use of time.
2   A number of existing training activities to continue, e.g. 'Time-Management' and 'Management of Change' courses.
3   A one-day workshop to be established on the topic of stress.
4   Guidance to be given on travel schedules, planning meetings, etc.
5   Medical screening to include assessment of mental health— and guidance to be given to those requiring assistance.
6   The match between people and jobs to be a priority. The personnel function to support this by continuing to improve selection and assessment techniques.
7   The annual appraisal mechanism to be used to review workload and draft individual development plans, such that

staff are given the opportunity to develop skills and acquire knowledge to match the demands of the job.

8 Managers to manage *people* as well as tasks and projects. They are in the ideal situation to help and support their staff. As individuals may, however, choose to seek the assistance of a counsellor outwith their normal sphere, the Personnel and Occupational Health functions should have sufficient trained people to meet this need. These counsellors must know when it is essential to refer individuals for more skilled or specialist support.

THE STRATEGY

Having determined the problems and possible solutions, the following set of aims was developed for a comprehensive stress management strategy (Table 8.3). A working group was set up to find ways to implement these aims, comprising representatives from Occupational Health, personnel and external advisers. The brief was to create a comprehensive approach to preventing, recognising and treating mental health problems of all levels of severity. The model shown in Table 8.3 appeared early in the discussions, and has proved a durable and self-explanatory schema.

This model consists of six levels. Most organisations fail to provide more than the first level of response, that is the physician and/or nurse recognising casualties and dealing with

Table 8.3 Stress management strategy

Levels	Aims	Facilitators
(1)	Treat casualties	Occupational Health Professionals
(2)	Detect other cases	Occupational Health Professionals/Managers
(3)	Legitimise stress	Senior Management
(4)	Increase awareness	Managers
		Training
		Occupational Health
(5)	Teach skills	Training
		Occupational Health
(6)	Improve culture	Total Organisation

them appropriately. This is a reactive response when presented with an anxious or distressed member of staff. Level 2 occurs when a more proactive approach is taken and early detection ensues, thus minimising morbidity. At stage 3, as has occurred in Zeneca Pharmaceuticals, the topic becomes a subject for legitimate discussion, that is stress-related conditions are seen as having the potential for disrupting efficiency and productivity.

If the most senior managers are able to accept the need for further action (level 4), increasing awareness of mental health and the need to maintain it, can drive a number of initiatives— one of which, level 5, is to ensure that skills in management of self and others is integrated into the company training programmes. Level 6 is the stage where the culture can begin to change to the benefit of individuals and the business performance itself.

The existing organisational management culture had previously been essentially a Type A, machismo-orientated approach to work where stress problems were usually concealed, and a complex mythology declared; for example, that a good manager is able to work effectively immediately after returning from a long-haul flight. A magical belief that increasing seniority should bring immunity from stress maintained these attitudes.

Paradoxically, the organisation was caring and supportive towards casualties, perhaps not least because of identification. Those who had required treatment for depression and anxiety usually received exemplary support, but this polarisation between those who had been affected by stress and a putative majority who had not, was in itself a stressor.

The belief engendered by some stress management consultants, and in particular training consultancies, that the effective teaching of stress management skills abolishes endogenous depression, anxiety, chemical dependence or normal adjustment reactions, leads to fragmented approaches to stress management without effective safety nets for those who require treatment.

For all of these reasons, it seemed essential as a first step that the subject should be legitimised, that senior management approval and participation should be sought from the outset, and that a continuation, or increase, in referrals for treatment should not be seen as a failure. Therefore the presentation to the Chairman and Board of Directors and the initiative which was started was a 'top-down' approach instituted from the beginning to communicate these key points.

The Chief Executive Officer's Letter

If stress management is to be effective, it must percolate into the informal culture of the organisation rather than just occupy the agenda of a few training sessions and then be forgotten. A pivotal step was the distribution to all departmental heads of a letter signed by the CEO. This reads as follows:

> I know that in recent months a number of Managers and employees have been concerned about the increasing demands of the business on employees and have seen this exemplified in a small but significant number of employees with serious problems.
>
> The business will continue to expand and it is important that appropriate pressure is placed on staff. Some stress is good for both individuals and the business leading to job satisfaction, motivation and good performance. Too much or inappropriate pressure on people who are unable to cope with it is bad for them and bad for the business.
>
> It is important for Managers to keep under surveillance the total workload on individuals and groups making sure that priorities and reasonable timescales are set. For example, I see it as important that staff have enough free time for outside pursuits. If work takes up more than a reasonable proportion of an individual's time, over too long a period, the business is unlikely to benefit in the long term. In this context an individual's holiday arrangements should only rarely be disrupted. The sensible planning and allocation of work within your departments is a vital factor in maximising efficiency. I would ask you to pay particular attention to staff whose duties oblige them to do a lot of travelling, and ensure that they plan their schedules in a sensible way.
>
> I have asked the Personnel and Occupational Health departments to pursue with you a number of detailed proposals designed to ensure a fuller appreciation of these issues and to minimise the incidence of stress-related problems in the organisation.

The letter led to a great deal of 'behind the scenes' discussion and support; not surprisingly some senior managers were threatened by the idea of employees apparently being told to work less hard and to consider their family and social lives as a high priority. In some quarters there was genuine fear that the commercial momentum of the organisation might be impaired. It will come as no surprise to those involved in organisational development work that this was not the case and indeed it seems likely that the reverse effect occurred. There is every indication that commitment and efficiency have improved; this is apparent from subjective reports, but more importantly is demonstrated by the continuing growth in profitability. There is no doubt, however that this letter, and the known existence of high-level working parties, increased interest and underlined credibility to all staff.

Stress Management Workshops

Agreement was reached that four pilot stress management workshops would be held. The objectives for the workshops were set as follows:

1   To raise awareness of what is meant by 'Stress'.
2   To legitimise Stress as a subject for discussion in the business.
3   To show a range of Stress Management skills with a view to further skills training.
4   To practise two key Stress Management skills, i.e. listening and relaxation.

The organisation and presentation of these workshops was a joint responsibility shared by the Training Section of Personnel and the Occupational Health Departments. The fact that this was the first such collaboration, and the knowledge that the participants for the first two workshops would include the Chairman and Board of Directors were in themselves stressors and the pre-workshop discussions were nervous and tentative, with considerable difficulty in agreeing the precise structure and content. It seems a universal paradox that stress management projects cause considerable stress for those designing and implementing them, perhaps partly because of the dynamics of allowing oneself to be seen as an 'expert' on stress who should, therefore, have no problems in dealing with it oneself. The open rejection of this myth at the beginning of every workshop relieves the tension for all involved.

A rudimentary attempt was made to evaluate the effectiveness of these early workshops by simple feedback questionnaires.

Pilot Stress Management Workshops

These were attended by 85% of all Directors, General Managers and Heads of Department.

Feedback questionnaires:

- 66% were in favour of the event as run
- 18% were broadly in favour
- 16% were critical

As a result of this initially encouraging feedback the Workshops were continued, and have evolved into a well-rehearsed event which is subjected to continual audit and development.

The workshops started in January 1988 and by the beginning of 1993 almost 700 individuals had attended. It was a deliberate policy to start at the top and work outwards—the first three workshops were attended by most of the Directors of the business.

The workshops began as a synthesis of information and skills training techniques drawn from management training and from the treatment of patients with stress problems. It became clear that the workshop model was an appropriate one, with group tasks and the sharing of experiences playing a vital part. Consideration of case studies, often only slightly modified from real life stories, provided a useful vehicle: these were originally presented on paper, then by role play using a professional actor, and then by the production of two high-quality videos depicting fictional case histories, which offer the benefits of reproducibility, dramatic interest, and realistic portrayal of a variety of familiar situations.

The idea behind the stress management workshop is relatively straightforward. It is to show that stress is a normal part of a healthy life which can, however, get out of control. It is important therefore to be able to recognise—in oneself and in others—when stress levels are becoming too great, and to do something about it before 'overload' is reached; that is, to learn 'stress management' skills. *The workshop is not intended to be a counselling forum for people who are deemed to have stress-related problems.* The workshop is spread over one full day with a further half day two months later. The organisers point out that participation in any workshop activity is voluntary and that all discussions are strictly confidential. As with most successful training programmes, the workshop involves a great deal of active participation. The day is relaxed and informal. The first exercise is simple and deceptively effective. Privately and in pairs, each participant spends 5 minutes telling their partner the sources of stress in their life. One person talks and the other listens. Roles are then reversed.

Back at base, everyone is asked in turn to describe what if any value such an exercise had but not to reveal the details. What emerges is surprisingly uniform; that there is a large degree of empathy—what stresses one person more often than not also stresses the other; and that simply to have someone who is patiently listening to you, and showing genuine interest in what you are saying, is in itself of immense value. Already, one hour into the day, one of the big barriers to success for stress management is crumbling. Stress is not confined to one or two individuals, and is a legitimate subject for discussion. A group 'brainstorming' session on the general topic of 'what stresses me' enables the course participants to focus more closely on those everyday strains which produce the symptoms of stress; late trains, cantankerous teenage children, prevaricating estate agents.

A specially commissioned video chronicles the events leading up to the nervous breakdown of John, a (fictitious) 'hard-pressed' ICI employee. In the ensuing discussion the events depicted are picked over with a fine-toothed comb. Why did he take on more work than he could handle? What was the responsibility of his boss? Could the signs have been spotted earlier? A second video shows how a different fictitious employee 'gets it right', and avoids the consequences of his unfortunate colleague. Finally, a brief introduction is given to various techniques of relaxation.

The Workshops Focus on the Four Key Areas where the Effects of Stress can be seen

This is best captured by reference to the model of Figure 8.2, which is extracted from the training guide.

The Distress Cycle

This is a model for demonstrating that increasing stress produces changes in four areas of human experience.

1 *Behavioural changes. Stress affects eating, drinking and smoking patterns and can make people restless and unable to settle. Some of us 'comfort eat' by nibbling at sweet and savoury snacks and then feeling guilty about it afterwards. Other people lose their appetite and become hungry and irritable. Alcohol is a very effective stress reducer, and is used on social occasions for precisely this reason. Our studies have shown that people smoke more and drink more when they are tense.*
2 *Physiological changes. The 'fight or flight' responses are activated. Heart rate and blood pressure go up, breathing rate and depth changes and blood is shunted away from non-urgent activities such as digestion and into muscles. This is very helpful at preparing the body to produce high physical output over the short term—and in*

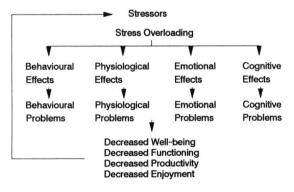

Figure 8.2 The distress cycle

doing so we 'burn off' the adrenalin. If carried on over a long period of time it can produce indigestion, fatigue and heart problems.

3   *Emotional changes. When stressed we feel irritable, anxious and restless—the experience that most people have had before an exam, an interview or a difficult meeting. Normally these feelings pass when we are distracted by the task in hand. If the stressors are less obvious, the feelings may become more permanent, making it difficult for the individual to sleep properly and to start the next day feeling refreshed and ready for action.*

4   *Cognitive changes. 'Cognitive' means to do with thinking functions. Stress can reduce concentration, make us feel that our memory is not working properly and reduce our capacity to take on the jobs we feel under pressure to complete.*

Any combination of these effects increases the stress load experienced by individuals and can create a vicious cycle.

The Wellness Cycle.

This cycle (Figure 8.3) introduces the concept of individuals developing skills to help them monitor feelings and behaviour in each of the four areas. If they can respond to stress by activating effective coping resources, then they can deal with the demands more effectively, thereby reducing their overall stress load.

The workshops present the theoretical basis for our behaviour patterns. They emphasise the benefits of the

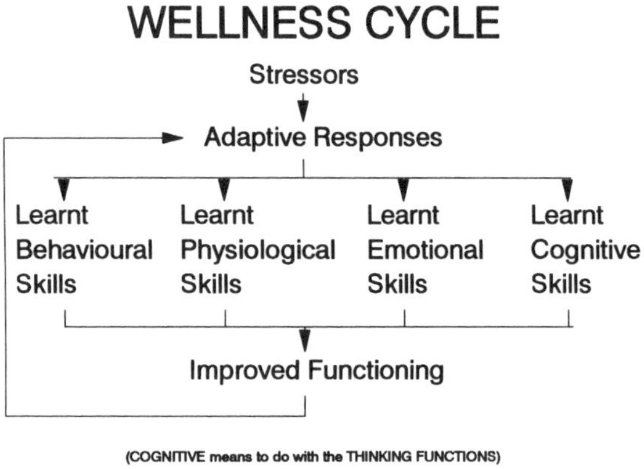

WELLNESS CYCLE

(COGNITIVE means to do with the THINKING FUNCTIONS)

Figure 8.3   *The wellness cycle*

practical development of specific skills which are based on the application of the wellness cycle to everyday life. These skills are best classified in the four areas introduced in the distress cycle.

1 *Behavioural skills.* Appropriate behavioural skills affect both work and social life. At work, the skills often included in management training such as time management, delegation, assertiveness and problem solving are effective here. Planned recreation and management of leisure and time with family and friends also receives specific attention.

   The development of these skills should result in increased self-esteem, enhanced self-respect and improved confidence.

2 *Physiological changes.* These include relaxation methods. The workshop includes practical experience of autogenic relaxation using the Jacobsen's Approach. There are, however, more than a dozen fundamentally different approaches to relaxation; it is emphasised that a 'one size fits all' approach may not be productive. Individuals are tasked to develop a relaxation method which works best for them.

   Adherence to a sensible lifestyle—including appropriate diet, adequate exercise and periods of rest—is essential to improve physical and mental health and resistance to disease.

3 *Emotional skills.* These overlap with behavioural skills, but counselling and active listening are used as working examples. In particular, the benefits of listening—as a human interaction rather than a prelude to managerial problem solving—are explained.

   Attention to improving the emotional elements of mental health should produce resilience and improving skills in handling future stressors.

4 *Cognitive skills.* The background to cognitive therapy is outlined in the workshops. Rational emotive therapy (RET) is used as a working example encouraging individuals to check, audit and review their personal belief systems. By this means, irrational beliefs such as perfectionism can be revealed and discussed.

   Acceptance of the world as it is and modifying behaviour to suit can be discussed.

DO THE WORKSHOPS PRODUCE
MEASURABLE BENEFITS?

Stress management initiatives such as this require a considerable investment of time, resources and effort. They are justifiable only if benefit can be demonstrated. The means to do this have been evolved as the workshops have been developed, but can be divided into three separate approaches.

Stress is hard to measure in absolute terms. Unlike other physical and physiological variables, there are no normative data. Measurement relies upon subjective reporting of unpleasant stress symptoms and experiences by using self-report questionnaires. We decided to ask workshop participants to complete questionnaires on a confidential basis. In a large study population, variations between individuals will tend to be smoothed out, but group average score changes will remain clear. What we are measuring is stress symptoms, not the level of stress in the organisation.

Validation Using Questionnaires

It was decided in 1989 to ask participants to complete questionnaires *before* attending the workshop and again *three months later*. Shortly after this component was added, a second half day was arranged as a review point at around this time, and has since become an integral part of the workshop activity. This provides an opportunity for individual feedback on questionnaire scores, a chance to review individual actions and plans and an opportunity to complete or reinforce any parts of the workshop which might need repetition.

Questionnaires used for this purpose had to meet the following criteria:

- Be concise enough to be completed in less than 30 minutes
- Be validated for test/retest reliability
- Normative data had to be available

We wished to quantify:

1 *Stress.* Suitable questionnaires were the Occupational Stress Indicator (OSI) and the General Health Questionnaire

(GHQ) in its 12, 28 and 30 item variants. The GHQ-30 was chosen in view of its suitability for such a workshop. The language, layout and time required for completion are appropriate, giving useful data without undue complexity. The GHQ provides a widely used and well-validated measure of self-reported stress symptoms. Higher scores indicate more symptoms.

2 *Coping.* The Social Adjustment Scale (SAS-M) Beliefs Inventory and various Locus of Control (LoC) scales were considered. The Nowicki and Strickland LoC scale was chosen.

Locus of Control offers the opportunity of quantifying the extent to which individuals feel in charge of their lifestyle and work situation. Although the concept is a rather loose one, it seemed a reasonable supposition that the development of stress management skills as described above might lead to individuals feeling more in control of their own destiny and health, and that this would be reflected in the change of the Locus of Control score. A disadvantage of using Locus of Control was the lack of 'user friendly' questionnaires which were appropriate to this population. The Nowicki and Strickland scale seemed the least unsuitable, but has not proved very acceptable.

Results

It must be emphasised that this is not a controlled study. Questionnaire data have been collected on more than 800 employees over six years, however, and the results are strikingly consistent.

GHQ Results

The way in which the information was collected is now displayed as follows:

1 Individuals completed the questionnaires prior to attending a stress management workshop and repeated the exercise approximately three months later. Average scores for those attending each workshop were plotted.

2   A line connecting the average GHQ scores for attendees measured *before* workshop attendance is shown on the following charts. Another line displays scores *approximately three months later* for the same groups of staff.

Figure 8.4 shows the scores for more than 50 workshops over a six-year period. The following three figures (Figures 8.5, 8.6, 8.7) depict the scores measured at the 'early' workshops (between 1988 and 1990), the 'mid-term' workshops conducted in 1990 and 1991, and the 'later workshops' during 1992 and 1993. As will be seen below, this highlights the trends measured in GHQ scores.

For most groups, the post-workshop scores were lower, indicating a reduction in self-reported stress symptoms. For each workshop the distribution of scores shows a 'bulge'

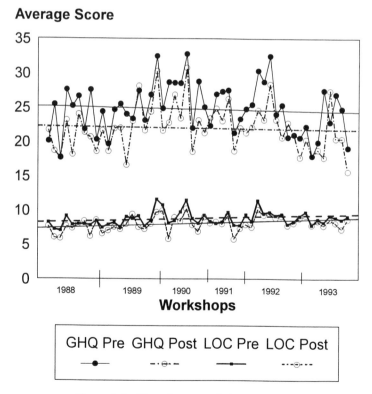

Figure 8.4   *Overview—workshops 1 to 51*

caused by the high scores of the subgroup who are experiencing high levels of stress at any given moment; their scores are strikingly high on occasion, and it is a chastening thought that some individuals in the workplace are admitting to more stress than patients being admitted to a psychiatric clinic. It seems unlikely that their work performance will be unaffected.

When retested between two and three months later, mean GHQ scores have fallen by 15–20%, and this improvement is demonstrated in those with normal, high or very high pre-workshop scores. This latter observation is very important,

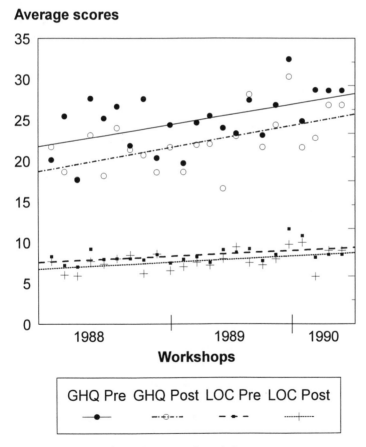

Figure 8.5 *Initial workshops*

since an effective intervention needs to reach the target group rather than simply preaching to the converted. By 'target group' we refer to those individuals with high GHQ scores, revealing substantial self-reported stress.

Stress levels within the organisation are high normal (mean GHQ 25.2) when compared with other occupational groups, such as commercial managers in other industries, pilots, military personnel. It will be noted that there is a consistently increasing trend in GHQ scores from the early days of the study through to late 1990 (Figure 8.5). GHQ scores fall following attendance at the workshop, although this might be expected since many stress symptoms are self-limiting.

The steady fall in LoC scores indicates a subjective increase in feelings of control and mastery over environment and circumstances. This is consistent with improved stress management skills. Figure 8.6 demonstrates that, after two years of project activity, in late 1989 we began to see that the rate of increase in measured stress levels began to flatten out.

It will be noted that, by late 1991, the measured benefit from workshop attendance as demonstrated by the gap between the GHQ Pre and GHQ Post scores was narrowing. The reader may wish to contemplate the possible reasons for this. One possibility considered was a reduction in effectiveness of the workshop, which was therefore reviewed. It is axiomatic that a workshop of this type must evolve in response to organisational change. Figure 8.7 demonstrates a continuation of the decreasing trend during the second half of 1992 and the beginning of 1993 in stress levels and a decreasing trend in scores.

If a trend line is plotted for the entire project, the lengthy increase is offset by the recent reduction in stress levels, producing an overall trend line which is remarkably flat (Figure 8.4). This is a striking result, which warrants further investigation. Comparable data from other organisations are not available, although anecdotal evidence and other studies suggest an increasing trend in stress levels generally. This would not be unexpected in view of the economic recession, political uncertainty and upheavals affecting most areas of human experience, from weather patterns and other natural disasters to social unrest.

Average Scores

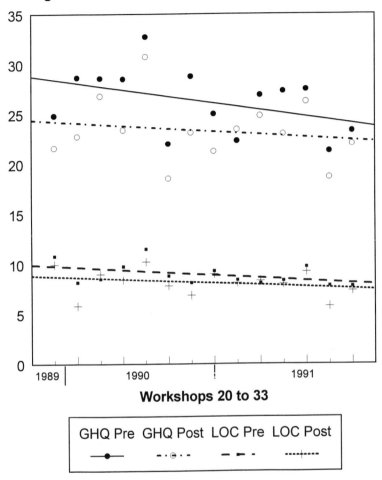

Workshops 20 to 33

GHQ Pre	GHQ Post	LOC Pre	LOC Post

Figure 8.6 *Mid-term results*

The figures demonstrate a measurable reduction in stress levels when questionnaires are repeated approximately two months after attendance at the workshop. However, this result must be treated with some caution since this study did not have the benefit of a control group. For these reasons the measurable reduction in GHQ scores suggests a significant improvement in stress management skills among workshop attendees despite an increase in the demands made on individuals.

Average Score

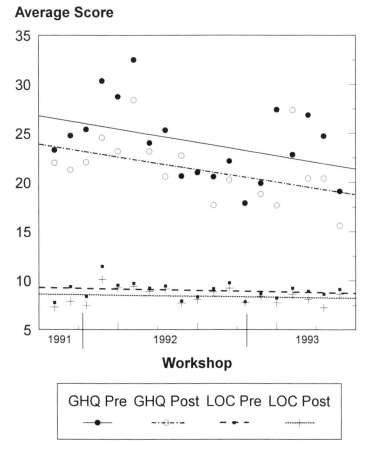

Figure 8.7 *Later workshops*

More focused study of the data produces some interesting results. The average pre-workshop score increased by 15% between 1988 and 1992, with noticeable increases at times of organisational stress such as the possible takeover threat in 1991. The possibility of demerger of ICI's Bioscience businesses into a new company caused uncertainty amongst staff during the second half of 1992. Detailed examination of stress management workshop scores during this time shows that stress levels rose—this would fit the psychological concept of 'anticipatory anxiety'.

The announcement of the formation of Zeneca was followed by a noticeable fall in scores. After the demerger took place stress levels declined, but it is noteworthy that the workshop which was occurring a few days after demerger revealed participants to have a higher GHQ score (indicating greater stress) after the workshop than beforehand. This phenomenon was also demonstrated at the time of the threatened takeover of ICI.

It is important when considering the above information to appreciate that the demands and pressures experienced by staff in the organisation have, if anything, risen since the mid 1980s. The above work indicates that self-reported stress symptoms have fallen over the last three years. This suggests, from the available data, that giving people skills to cope with busy demanding lives is an effective policy and should be sustained.

Locus of Control Results

Pre-workshop assessment of Locus of Control scores reveals a strongly 'internal' average score. This suggests that the members of staff assessed felt able to influence, and be responsible for, events occurring around them. This is consistent with the culture of a science-based, commercial organisation. It should be remembered that 'internal' scores can predispose to stress; scores seemed to differ amongst departments and job roles as would be expected, and there was no significant change at follow-up.

With the benefit of hindsight, Locus of Control could have been omitted in favour of measuring Beliefs Systems, Assertiveness or Type A behaviours (of which there were many striking examples amongst workshop participants); the constraint of time available for the completion and analysis of questionnaires was, as always, a serious limitation.

Number of Cases Presenting

Overall, the number of people presenting with stress-related illness has fallen. Figure 8.8 displays the number of individuals who needed to be referred to psychiatrists or psychologists or who had attended the ICI Medical Centres or their own family

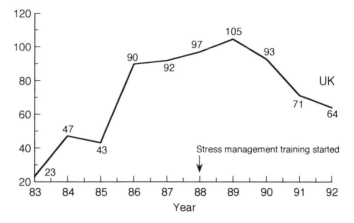

Figure 8.8   *Referrals to psychiatrists or psychologists; attendance at Zeneca Pharmaceuticals medical centres or family doctors' clinics*

doctors' clinics over the last 10 years. We can reasonably assume that this results from improved *earlier intervention* as average GHQ scores from the workshops held in recent years indicate increasing subjective stress levels. There is a striking parallel between self-reported prevalence of stress symptoms from the GHQ studies (Figures 8.4–8.7) and the above 'casualty' figures, that is, both start with a rising trend which is controlled and reversed.

Individual Feedback

Comment from individuals attending workshops continues to be positive. Individuals report a much greater awareness of the demands placed on them and how they can best organise their work, domestic and social lives to increase efficiency and enjoyment. Demand for places on the workshops remains high and the training is seen as a part of essential management training. The workshops have also helped to identify wider training needs such as the development of improved skills in assertiveness, time management, and so on.

The 'Getting It Right' package, including literature, tapes and videos, has been formatted for ease of use throughout both

ICI and Zeneca. It has been welcomed by many other organisations, institutions, Health Authorities and Health Care providers, not only in the UK but internationally.

There is clear evidence from the data available, all of which supports our observations that:

1 Stress levels within the organisation are high.
2 Some individuals are adversely affected by stress.
3 The interventions described above, especially the Stress Management Workshops, are effective in reducing symptoms reported and restoring function quickly.

The project continues, and a current objective is to refine and extend the assessments, preferably by including a control group.

ANALYSIS OF BENEFIT

Traditionally, much of the justification for stress management training has been based on increased subjective well-being. However, since the mid 1980s a growing body of research has demonstrated objective improvement in cardio-vascular health resulting from behaviour modification, including relaxation training, as a first-line treatment for hypertension in general practice (Patel & Marmot, 1988), and in improving outcome for post-myocardial infarct patients (Friedman, Thoresen, Gill et al., 1986; Ornish, Brown, Scherwitz et al., 1990).

There is also a need to evaluate cost benefit in terms of employee productivity, employee turnover, and sickness and absence rates. This, however, is notoriously difficult to do with any accuracy because of the number of complicating factors which prevent the assumption of a fixed base line.

Although the development of the project was empirical, its key aims are supported by the draft proposals established by the United States National Institute of Occupational Safety and Health in 1986 which were:

- Attention to job design
- Improved surveillance
- Improved training, transfer of information and resource development

- An enriched mental health component within industry (occupational) health services

The *ICI–Zeneca Pharmaceuticals strategy* was carefully thought out and based on the following elements:

1 Early involvement of Directors and General Managers.
2 Collaboration between Occupational Health, Training, Organisational experts and managers.
3 Effective communication with managers regarding the importance of mental health and stress.
4 The adoption of suitable parameters to quantify the business position.
5 The introduction of well-planned, professional training and educational programmes, including skills training workshops.
6 The evolution of a finely tuned, validated workshop, based around two high quality videos.
7 Effective publicity with the production of leaflets, booklets and other educational training aids.
8 A complementary counselling and treatment service.
9 Monitoring, using appropriate measures, to assess the benefits of the above initiatives.
10 The implementation of a cultural change initiative within the business leading to better development of individuals and targeting of organisational efforts to agreed goals.

Much of the work in ICI–Zeneca has been focused on managers. They are the people who usually determine the culture and in whom the organisation has invested more heavily. Ideally a stress management initiative should take account of the needs of staff at *all* levels. Whilst the 'stressors' may be different, there is substantial evidence that most people within an organisation are at risk. Alternative training and educational activities have been tailored within ICI–Zeneca for specific needs, such as dedicated sessions for secretarial and administrative staff and supervisors. It was appreciated that support staff might often be the ones to whom tasks are delegated. They, just as importantly, need coping skills. There is, however, key basic information which should be familiar to *all* staff. This can best be presented in purpose-designed booklets and fact sheets.

SUMMARY

Defining objectives and accountability clearly, setting priorities and managing time effectively are essential. In an innovative and demanding environment, maintaining the health of staff and managing stress positively is likely to improve productivity, reduce errors, increase creativity, improve decision making and lead to enhanced job satisfaction.

A policy for mental health is not a 'stand alone' initiative, but part of an integrated approach to managing a high quality organisation. The challenge in any organisation, is to allow and encourage an appropriate amount of stress or pressure to enhance the performance of individuals, the departments where they work and thus the business and organisation as a whole.

REFERENCES

Cooper, C. L. & Marshall, J. (1980). *White Collar and Professional Stress*. Chichester & New York: Wiley.

Friedman, M., Thoresen, C. E., Gill, J. J., Ulmer, D., Powell, L. H., Price, V. A., Brown, B., Thompson, L., Rabin, D. D., Breall, W. S., Bourg, E., Levy, R. & Dixon, T. (1986). Alteration of type A behavior and its effect on cardiac recurrences in post-myocardial infarction patients: Summary results of the recurrent coronary prevention project. *American Heart Journal*, **12**, No. 4, 653–665.

Goldberg, D. (1972). *The Detection of Psychiatric Illness by Questionnaire*. Oxford: Oxford University Press.

Ornish, D., Brown, S. E., Scherwitz, L. W., Billings, J. H., Armstrong, W. T., Ports, T. A., McLanahan, S. M., Kirkeeide, R. L., Brand, R. J. & Lance Gould, K. (1990). Can lifestyle changes reverse coronary heart disease? The lifestyle Heart Trial. *Lancet*, **336**, 129–133.

Patel, C. & Marmot, M. (1988). Can general practitioners use training in relaxation and management of stress to reduce mild hypertension? *British Medical Journal*, **296**, 21–24.

9
Caring for the Carers: North Derbyshire Health Authority

PETER LEAKEY, MATHEW LITTLEWOOD
Department of Clinical Psychology, North Derbyshire
Health Authority
SHIRLEY REYNOLDS, DAVID BUNCE
MRC/ESRC Social and Applied Psychology Unit,
University of Sheffield

INTRODUCTION

Health care staff provide services which promote the physical and psychological health of the population. What services are provided to this large group of employees to promote their well-being and effectiveness at work? This chapter outlines some of the initiatives taken in North Derbyshire Health Authority (NDHA) which have the well-being of health care staff as their focus.

The aim of the British National Health Service (NHS) is to provide a comprehensive health care service to the population of the UK. The NHS employs just under 1 000 000 people in a range of professional, administrative, managerial and ancillary

Creating Healthy Work Organizations. Edited by C. L. Cooper and S. Williams.
© 1994 John Wiley & Sons Ltd

positions which makes it the largest employing organisation in the UK (Levitt & Wall, 1992). Recently there has been increasing awareness that the health and well-being of NHS employees may be a critical factor in the effective delivery of health services. For example, the Department of Health has recently commissioned a series of studies concerned with improving the psychological well-being of the NHS workforce.

At a more local level individual Health Authorities have, to varying degrees, recognized the importance of providing direct services to employees which attempt to promote their psychological and physical well-being. Within North Derbyshire Health Authority this recognition has resulted in a series of coordinated initiatives under the title 'Caring for the Carers'. These range from providing individual counselling for staff with psychological problems, to working with teams and groups to improve the functioning and effectiveness of the work team. In this chapter our aim is to describe the evolution and achievements of these varied initiatives and to evaluate the extent to which these have influenced the organizational management of employee well-being.

Organizational Context

Although there are considerable conceptual, methodological and empirical problems in stress and burnout research (Handy, 1988; Reynolds & Shapiro, 1991), one achievement of this huge research area appears to be the increasing acceptance by workers and employers that there may be a relationship between the nature of work and work environments and the psychological well-being, physical health and even effectiveness of workers. For example, Jones, Barge, Steffy et al. (1988) reported that levels of strain in health care staff were positively correlated with the number of medication errors that were made.

An ever increasing volume of research suggests that health care workers experience specific job-related difficulties and report elevated levels of psychological disorders compared with other working groups (Firth & Britton, 1989; Firth, 1986; Payne & Firth-Cozens, 1987; Rees & Cooper, 1990). Factors such as sickness absence and turnover may also indicate high levels of dissatisfaction or high levels of physical and psychological strain (Firth & Britton, 1989). There are a number of features of health care work which may give rise to psychological strain amongst employees. For example, the nature of health care work and the inevitable contact with, and treatment of, chronically ill people, places emotional burdens on staff (Cooper & Mitchell, 1990). In addition, health care work, like many other forms of work, has been subject to continued technological changes both in treatment delivery and in routine administration. Finally, the NHS has been subject to continual reorganization and restructuring with major organizational changes introduced in 1974, 1982 and 1989.

Although these various difficulties have been increasingly acknowledged informally, there are few recorded formal attempts to provide support services for staff. The work described in this chapter has been conducted within a District Health Authority. It began in 1986 and has been maintained and developed since that time with some support from the Regional Health Authority. In 1986 a number of key departments within North Derbyshire Health Authority began to recognize that staff members were increasingly presenting themselves for help with personal difficulties. In response to these difficulties a number of strategies were offered on an ad hoc basis. For example, the Clinical Psychology Department began to offer stress management training courses to staff and to provide therapy and counselling to staff, the Occupational Health Department and the Hospital Chaplain were offering staff support in informal ways, and the Health Promotion Department were attempting to establish health promotion initiatives with staff such as healthy eating and stress management techniques.

In recognition of these independent initiatives the Personnel Department established a forum for the coordination and integration of these varied groups. The District Stress Working Group was established with representation from each of the following departments: Personnel, Occupational Health, Health Promotion, Clinical Psychology and the Chaplaincy. Since that original initiative in 1986, the Stress Working Group have established and developed a range of strategies for promoting staff well-being. These include conducting a survey of psychological well-being amongst staff, setting up a staff counselling service, providing stress management training to a wide range of professional groups, developing a psychological debriefing service for staff involved with victims of trauma and disasters, training staff to introduce innovation techniques in their work, and working as consultants to multidisciplinary staff groups. Wherever possible these initiatives have been evaluated through collaboration with the support of colleagues at the Social and Applied Psychology Unit (SAPU) and this emphasis on evaluation has added greatly to the credibility of the varied initiatives.

OVERVIEW OF OCCUPATIONAL STRESS INTERVENTION STRATEGIES

Reviews of occupational stress interventions typically distinguish between three classes of intervention: those interventions which focus on individual workers and their ability to cope with work demands, those which intervene at the group level, and those which attempt to change the organization or the nature of jobs themselves (DeFrank & Cooper, 1987; Ivancevich, Matteson, Freedman & Phillips, 1990; Newman & Beehr, 1979). There appears to be a consensus in the literature that individually oriented methods such as stress management training and counselling have been favoured in research and practice, and that there is a compelling case for developing group- and organizational-level interventions. In addition, many authors have recommended that the choice of intervention strategy should be explicitly guided by prior assessment of the organization and its members (Hurrell & Murphy, 1987, Ivancevich & Matteson, 1987).

SURVEY OF PSYCHOLOGICAL WELL-BEING AMONGST STAFF

One of the initial priorities of the Stress Working Group was to prepare a report for senior managers in the Health Authority which would set out the aims of the group and the nature of the problems which they were attempting to alleviate, and make recommendations for management action. The recommendations of this report were based in part on the results of a questionnaire survey of staff. The questionnaire was sent to a 1 in 7 sample of all NDHA employees and 303 employees (47% of the sample) returned their questionnaires. It consisted of a brief, anonymous questionnaire which included an established measure of psychological well-being (the 12-item General Health Questionnaire, GHQ-12: Goldberg, 1972), a section concerned with perceived sources of stress, and a checklist of stress-related behaviours.

The results of this survey provided a more substantive basis for the concerns of the Working Group. Staff were classified according to broad employment categories as defined by the Whitley Council: nursing and midwifery, medical and dental, administrative and clerical, ancillary staff, maintenance and other professional and technical groups. The response rate of these different groups varied widely but indicated that some groups appeared to experience high levels of psychological disorder. The GHQ-12 can be scored to indicate levels of psychological distress and to identify which respondents are probable 'cases' (i.e. that their psychological difficulties are of a serious nature). For example, amongst the 165 nurses and midwives who responded, 46.7% were classified as a possible 'case'.

Recommendations to Senior Management

These findings provided the basis of a report and recommendations to senior management which was presented in 1987. The recommendations made at that time were as follows.

1 Develop a long-term multilevel strategy for promoting staff well-being, including:

(a) management training to enhance stress awareness;

(b) developing the climate and structure of the organization to facilitate organizational solutions to stress problems (e.g. quality circles, staff reviews, participative management, team briefing);

(c) preventive programmes promoting general health and stress management skills;

(d) remedial activities (e.g. a counselling service, staff support groups).

2 Highlight the Health Authority's concern for, and the value placed on, employees. Take a lead in promoting greater awareness and understanding of work stress at all levels of the organization.

3 Unit General Managers should investigate worksites showing the greatest levels of psychological distress and generate specific action plans.

4 All managers should be explicitly encouraged to generate strategies for reducing work stress within the part of the organization over which they are responsible.

5 Stress levels should be monitored regularly to help evaluate the outcomes of intervention strategies.

6 Training needs of staff should be given high priority.

7 A system of staff review should be developed throughout the Health Authority.

8 Local resources should be used to provide a range of health promoting activities for staff (e.g. yoga, relaxation, aerobics, meditation).

The report of the Stress Working Group was received cautiously by senior managers. Not surprisingly, given the nature of the recommendations made and the sensitive nature of the survey results there was some reluctance to make the document public. This reluctance was reflected in the ambiguous status given to the report and recommendations; senior managers agreed to remove the confidential status of the document but it was not formally distributed to staff. However, the initial impact of the report was sufficient to provide a catalyst for more direct and coordinated efforts to introduce interventions to improve staff well-being.

THE STAFF COUNSELLING SERVICE

The staff counselling service began in 1986. Since that time the service has been provided from within existing resources and 22 staff with training in counselling or psychological therapies from the departments of clinical psychology, psychiatric nursing, occupational health and the chaplaincy act as staff counsellors. Each of these counsellors accepts a limited number of staff clients in addition to their normal work duties. The principles of the counselling service were established at the outset and publicized through the staff newsletter. The service is offered free of charge and on a confidential basis to all employees of the health service. Further information about the service and about the counsellors has been provided through posters and leaflets and, increasingly, through reputation and word of mouth. Employees refer themselves to the service and are seen within five days of this initial contact.

There are a number of advantages in using a large number of staff counsellors. Firstly, the service can be flexible and responsive without placing excessive demands on any one counsellor; secondly, counsellors are geographically dispersed throughout the Health Authority which enables prospective clients easy access to a local counsellor wherever their worksite may be; finally, this geographical dispersion and the large number of counsellors ensure that staff can contact a staff counsellor whom they will not ordinarily meet in their day-to-day work.

The original intention was to coordinate access and referrals to staff counsellors through the Occupational Health Department. This would facilitate monitoring and evaluation of the service and enable referrals to be allocated according to workload. This centralized approach was, however, circumvented by staff who began to approach counsellors directly as their identities became known.

The introduction of counselling services at work has been increasing in the UK but evaluation is still uncommon and staff attitudes to such services have not been explored. One potential problem which may inhibit staff use of worksite counselling services is the negative image which is held of individuals who seek professional psychiatric or psychological help (Parish & Kappes, 1979; Sibicky & Davidio, 1986). There is some evidence that individuals who themselves work in a helping profession may be more than usually resistant to acknowledging their own psychological difficulties and more concerned with the potential stigma associated with using counselling or psychotherapy. In order to examine these issues, in 1989 a study of staff attitudes to the counselling service was undertaken in conjunction with SAPU at the University of Sheffield (West & Reynolds, 1993).

Questionnaires were sent anonymously to a 1 in 7 sample of NDHA employees and 44% were returned. The results of this study established that despite numerous attempts to publicize the service through the staff newsletter, posters and word of mouth, just over half (55%) of the sample were aware that a staff counselling service existed and only a quarter (25%) knew how to contact the service should they need to. In general, attitudes towards counselling were positive although a majority of respondents (64%) agreed that they would be embarrassed if they used the service and if other colleagues found out about this. Perceptions of managers' attitudes towards the counselling service were more neutral. Much less positive were respondents' beliefs that confidentiality of clients would be maintained.

Regression analysis was used to predict attitudes to the counselling service. Positive attitudes to the NDHA counselling service were predicted by confidence in the confidentiality of the service and positive attitudes towards clients of counselling services. In other words, those employees who believed that confidentiality could be maintained and who rated potential clients as trustworthy and effective were more likely to have favourable attitudes towards the service.

These results highlight the importance of promoting positive images of worksite counselling services and of those who use them. There is, in many organizations, a fear that rumour and gossip will sabotage confidentiality and a fear that those who use the service will be perceived as unable to cope and that their future career development will suffer. In organizations such as the health service where the counselling is provided by other employees of the organization one can see how such fears can flourish.

Despite these barriers to using the service, increasing numbers of staff are referring themselves each year. Between January and December 1987 a total of 40 clients were seen by the staff counsellors. Between January 1992 and December 1992 this had risen to 206 clients seen in 576 sessions. There is evidence that many of these clients are presenting with severe psychological difficulties, similar to those presented in adult mental health settings. This can be illustrated by examining the presenting problems of 37 staff clients seen by one counsellor during an eleven-month period (Table 9.1). The range of difficulties presented by health service employees are clearly greater than those specifically concerned with work-related problems and in fact represent problems typical of those in standard out-patient settings. This range and potential severity of problems makes it essential that counsellors are experienced and skilled and that they have access to regular supervision.

There is a clear need for workplace counselling services to be rigorously evaluated. Despite the increased numbers of such services in the UK and USA, controlled outcome studies are rare (Berridge & Cooper, 1993; Swanson & Murphy, 1991). One of the reasons for the general lack of evaluation may be the overwhelming need for counsellors to guarantee confidentiality and the belief that this could be compromised by research

Table 9.1 *Staff referrals seen by one counsellor from February 1990 to December 1990*

Presenting problem	No. of referrals
Stress symptoms	10
Depression	8
Complicated grief	5
Phobia	1
Smoking cessation	2
Marital problems	1
Post-traumatic stress disorder	2
Psychosomatic symptoms	1
Childhood sexual abuse	2
Panic attacks	3
Alcohol problems	1
Chronic pain	1

demands. The efficacy of the NDHA counselling service (recently named RESOLVE) is currently being assessed in conjunction with colleagues from SAPU. One of the future priorities of the NDHA counselling service is to establish a method for assessing the efficacy of the service. Aside from any scientific reasons for conducting such an evaluation there are increasing internal demands for health service funded work to demonstrate that it is cost-effective.

STRESS MANAGEMENT TRAINING

Stress management training (SMT) has become a common workplace intervention which aims to assist employees in the management of demanding work environments by imparting a range of skills and techniques. These techniques are most commonly based on cognitive-behavioural psychotherapy and usually involve some combination of relaxation training, self-management skills such as time management and goal setting, and cognitive techniques such as reappraisal (Beck, 1976; Kahn & Byosiere, 1992; Meichenbaum, 1985). A key distinction between counselling approaches and SMT is that SMT is offered primarily as a preventive strategy, to workers who have not been identified as experiencing high levels of psychological distress.

Results of the staff survey indicated that large numbers of staff, particularly those in nursing and midwifery, reported above-average levels of psychological distress. In health care organizations, nurses and midwives are typically the single largest group of employees and are responsible for a substantial proportion of direct patient care. For these reasons this group were targeted as a priority for intervention. Preliminary work within the Psychology Department involved the development of a structured stress management training programme. Members of the department were assigned to research specific stress management techniques and to develop these into a self-contained teaching module. Subsequently, presentations of theory and demonstrations of appropriate teaching methods and resources were given to the department as a whole to develop basic levels of skills within department staff.

Once the stress management training package had been developed the next stage of developing the service to staff was to target specific occupational groups and to secure the support of senior managers of these staff. In order to do this Nursing Officers were the first group to whom the stress management training programme was offered. These initial training sessions were well attended and provided a means of securing access to other less senior members of the nursing group and other professional groups such as physiotherapists and occupational therapists.

The delivery of stress management training is flexible and responsive to the specific needs and constraints of different groups such as shift working and the flexibility of work rotas. Training has been offered in weekly sessions, one-day and two-day packages and usually lasts for approximately 15 hours in total. The content of workshops is also influenced by the specific needs of occupational groups.

Contents of Stress Management Training

Stress management training has developed as a generic package of education and self-management skills based on the principles and practice of cognitive behaviour therapy. In format stress management training is usually highly participative and responsive, and teaching methods rely heavily on experiential exercises, group discussions and the exploration of personal needs. There are a number of key areas which can be combined to make up a comprehensive training package.

1 *General information about stress.* This provides a basic understanding of the psychological and physiological basis of stress and its causes and effects in everyday life. Participants are encouraged to consider and discuss their own experiences to help them recognize the signs and sources of their own stress.

2 *Relaxation methods.* Participants are encouraged to develop existing methods of relaxation and to develop new skills. Relaxation training is given which can include deep muscular relaxation, meditation or massage. Participants

are encouraged to practise these methods regularly and are given repeated opportunities within the training programme to practise them within sessions.

3   *Handling relationships.* Relationships are seen as a primary source of satisfaction and stress. Relationships include those at work with colleagues, superiors and subordinates, relationships with patients or clients, and personal relationships with family members and friends. In discussing this area participants are introduced to theoretical and skills-based models of how relationships work, how problems arise, and new strategies for improving interactions with other people. Skills such as assertiveness and negotiation may be demonstrated and practised. In addition participants are encouraged to assess and develop their own social support networks.

4   *Thinking and stress.* This helps participants to understand the role of thinking in the experience of stress. It examines the way in which the interpretations that we make for everyday events can differ and how these interpretations influence our emotional states and physical responses. Participants are shown ways of modifying their own thinking processes and how they can challenge and modify thoughts, interpretations and beliefs that contribute to their experiences of stress.

5   *Time management.* Ways of managing time to meet varied work and non-work demands are examined. Participants are encouraged to consider their work and personal life goals and to prioritize these.

6   *Understanding and handling emotions.* This area aims to help participants understand and handle strong emotional states in themselves and others. This can include sessions on dealing with anger or with grief or basic counselling skills. Participants are encouraged to consider ways of identifying stress in other people.

In addition to these components several themes are presented throughout the training course. General problem solving skills as applied to current organizational or work issues are demonstrated and discussed and participants are encouraged to practise their relaxation skills and given tasks to complete between sessions.

Evaluating Stress Management Training

Published reports evaluating stress management training typically demonstrate that participants experience improvements in levels of psychological symptoms such as depression and anxiety and reductions in physiological indices of strain such as blood pressure (Bruning & Frew, 1987; Ganster, Mayes, Sime & Tharp, 1982; Murphy, 1984, 1988). One issue which has arisen, however, in the evaluation and development of these courses is the extent to which benefits to individuals are related to the varied components of the training course. For example, Sallis, Trevorrow, Johnson, Hovell and Kaplan (1987) compared three different programmes, one involving a varied combination of different strategies, another which was specifically concerned with relaxation training and a third, minimal intervention, consisting of education and support only. To the authors' surprise all three programmes resulted in similar benefits to the participants. This finding led them to suggest that the benefits derived from stress management training may be unrelated to the specific skills that participants learn and instead related to more general factors such as the support offered by a group and the chance to discuss difficulties with other colleagues.

In order to evaluate the stress management training offered to NDHA staff a collaborative research project was initiated with researchers from SAPU. Informal feedback had indicated that training was greatly valued by staff but there had been little formal evaluation of the programmes. The collaborative project had two main aims, first to assess the general level of benefit to participants, and secondly to establish if different components of training had specific effects on participants and were related to improvements in their well-being at the end of training and three months after training.

The study focused on 10 stress management training groups which were presented to staff in six weekly sessions each of two hours. A total of 92 female staff took part in the study; they were between 22 and 63 years old (mean age 39.7 years) and had worked for the health authority for an average of 7.5 years. The content of training was intended to represent typical multimodal stress management training. In order to examine the specific impacts of different techniques each weekly session was devoted to new material which was presented in a predetermined order and followed the outline of stress management training described above. In order to establish the overall effects of training the ten training groups were randomly allocated to immediate training in autumn 1989 or delayed training in spring 1990. Measures of psychological well-being, job satisfaction and non-job satisfaction were completed by participants before training, one month after training and three months after training. The specific impacts of each training session and each topic were assessed by having participants complete brief questionnaires after each session. These questionnaires tapped participants' general evaluations of the sessions in terms of their post-session mood and more specific impacts concerned with the content of sessions; for example, specific things that participants had learned which we called 'task' impacts or the emotional support from the group which we call 'interpersonal' impacts.

There were clear effects of the training course on employees' psychological well-being but not on their job satisfaction or non-job satisfaction. The full set of assessment questionnaires were completed by 62 participants and their data were used to evaluate the outcomes of the training. Table 9.2 shows levels of psychological well-being and job and non-job satisfaction at the varied assessment points. Prior to either group receiving training (Time 1) levels of psychological well-being were identical in the two groups. Statistical tests indicated that participants' well-being after training was significantly higher than at pre-training and that this benefit was maintained at three month follow-up. Participants reported that at three months after the end of training they continued to use practical skills they had learned on the courses such as relaxation training and time management.

The impact of session contents conformed to one of two patterns. There was evidence that different components of stress management training had specific immediate effects on participants. For example, participants reported that they had significantly higher levels of personal insight after session 2 which dealt with relaxation, session 3 which dealt with relationships and session 4 which dealt with ways of thinking.

Table 9.2 *Means and standard deviations of psychological distress, job satisfaction and non-job satisfaction at Time 1 to Time 4*

	Time 1		Time 2		Time 3		Time 4	
	Immed. (n = 32)	Delay (n = 30)	Immed. (n = 32)	Delay (n = 30)	Immed. (n = 32)	Delay (n = 30)	Immed.	Delay (n = 30)
Psychological distress	12.10	12.10	11.06	13.97	11.03	10.37	N/A	9.85
(SD)	(4.70)	(4.54)	(5.71)	(5.89)	(4.24)	(5.27)		(4.12)
Job satisfaction	2.80	2.98	2.89	3.02	2.80	3.06	N/A	3.01
(SD)	(0.87)	(0.86)	(0.85)	(0.76)	(0.89)	(0.70)		(0.73)
Non-job satisfaction	2.59	2.84	2.46	2.92	2.41	2.74	N/A	2.72
(SD)	(1.18)	(0.80)	(1.13)	(1.01)	(1.21)	(1.02)		(1.04)

Note: Immediate group had stress management training between Time 1 and Time 2; delayed group had training between Time 2 and Time 3.

Personal insight was significantly lower after the first, introductory session. Similarly, participants reported higher levels of awareness after session 4 (ways of thinking) than they did after the first (introductory) session or session 5 (time management).

There was also evidence that training had more general non-specific effects on participants. This was indicated by smooth and statistically significant trends reported between sessions 1 to 6. For example, participants' problem definition ratings and problem solution ratings increased in a smooth, linear trend. We interpreted these results as representing incremental learning over the course of the training. Similarly, ratings of feeling supported or relieved by sessions increased over time, indicating that participants were more supported and relieved after later sessions. These results were interpreted as indicating greater group cohesion as the training proceeded which reflected the development of group processes (Reynolds, Taylor & Shapiro, 1993).

In addition to examining the general effects of the training programme and the specific effects of each weekly session we examined the extent to which each session contributed to the overall benefits experienced by participants. Ratings of session impacts were averaged over the six sessions and correlated with post-training well-being and satisfaction. After controlling for differences between participants before training, only positive mood after the sessions predicted psychological well-being after training. Ratings of all the task and interpersonal impacts were significantly correlated with non-job satisfaction at the end of training; more positive ratings of these impacts after each training session were associated with greater non-job satisfaction one month after training. Three months after training, however, most of these associations were no longer significant.

In contrast to the average level of session impacts we also assessed the effects of changes in participants' evaluation of sessions. As described earlier, problem definition and problem solution, support and relief all increased linearly over the course of the six training sessions. We calculated the rate of this increase (the slope) and examined the extent to which the slope was related to post-training outcomes. Our results indicated that the rate of change was significantly associated with psychological well-being at the end of training; thus those participants whose problem solving and ratings of support and relief increased during the six sessions were more likely to report greater psychological well-being at the end of training (Reynolds, Taylor & Shapiro, in press).

These results have practical implications for the future development and delivery of workplace stress management training. In addition to the importance of specific skills training it seems clear that participants greatly valued and benefited from the structured and supportive context of the training sessions. Thus, those participants who reported that support and relief increased during the six training sessions were those who also reported the most improved psychological well-being. This suggests that providers of stress management training should focus on the processes of training in addition to the contents and methods of training. An additional and important finding was that session impacts were related to non-work satisfaction. This might suggest that the techniques that were taught were particularly applicable outside the workplace. The focus of occupational stress research has often obscured the fact that most workers have important social roles outside work and that for women in particular, there may be a great need to balance the demands of their work and domestic lives.

ORGANIZATIONAL-FOCUSED STRESS MANAGEMENT INTERVENTIONS

The main feature of the interventions described earlier (counselling and stress management training) is that they target individual employees by attempting to enhance their ability to cope with work-related strain. A contrasting approach to stress management is to target environmental or organizational factors giving rise to occupational strain. Several reviews have drawn attention to the need to evaluate such interventions (e.g. DeFrank & Cooper, 1987; Murphy, 1984, 1988) which broadly address either interpersonal, intra- and intergroup processes, or techno-structural features such as work design, organizational structure, information and reward systems (Beer & Walton, 1990). Such organizational-focused approaches to stress management can be initiated in two ways: either external agencies identify aspects of the workplace requiring remedial attention and then implement appropriate procedures to reduce associated work strain, or the workforce themselves undertake this process.

The intervention described in this section adopted the latter approach, where health care workers attended a programme designed to help identify work-based stressors, and then to tackle these through *innovative coping*. Innovative coping refers to the introduction of new skills or procedures designed to significantly benefit the individual or their work group by modifying or alleviating recognized work stressors. For example, this might involve the introduction of new working methods where troublesome procedures are updated, rearranging work schedules, introducing means of enhancing working relations between individuals and groups, or modifying the physical work environment.

What grounds are there for believing the promotion of innovative coping may benefit workers? Theoretically, it is desirable that stress management programmes encourage a balanced approach to coping where individuals learn not only how to deal with the manifestations of work-related strain, but also how to tackle the underlying stressor directly. Innovative coping is central to the latter approach. Empirically, no research has specifically looked at innovative coping, although managers who have the opportunity to be creative and to decide their own working procedures report greater satisfaction and appear better adjusted than those who do not have such opportunities (Nicholson & West, 1988). Among Health Visitors, innovation has been positively associated with workload (West, 1989) although the direction of causality is not clear. Practically, the development and modification of working procedures associated with innovative coping, in addition to improving psychological well-being, is also likely to result in enhanced productivity and quality of work.

Comparing Innovation Training and Stress Management Training

In the present study an intervention designed to promote

innovative coping was contrasted with a control group and with a modified stress management training group. In order to maximize the differences between the innovation training and the stress management training group some aspects of stress management training were modified in this study. In particular, training in problem solving skills which was most similar to the content of innovation training was excluded from the stress management training programmes. In addition to addressing the need to develop and empirically evaluate organizational-focused stress management interventions in relation to individual-focused programmes, the study also possessed the following features. Many studies have restricted themselves to a narrow range of outcome variables which are unlikely to capture all the psychological dimensions potentially influenced by stress management interventions. Thus, outcome measures were selected which assessed not only psychological strain (work-related and general), but also indices of psychological well-being (job satisfaction and motivation), and work-based innovation. Furthermore, many studies have restricted their follow-up period to three months, thereby giving no indication of the long-term benefits of such programmes. The present study therefore, assessed follow-up five months and one year following the interventions.

It was expected that both stress management training and innovation training would improve psychological well-being and reduce strain. Due to the time required to initiate and implement innovations, a delay was expected in the innovation promotion programme before increased levels of innovation were apparent. As suggested by other organizational-focused interventions (Wall & Clegg, 1981), it was expected that associated improvements in psychological strain and well-being would also take longer in this condition.

In order to compare the effects of innovation training, stress management training and no training, staff were allocated to one of these three conditions on the basis of their work location: 66 staff were allocated to stress management training, 52 to innovation training, and 83 acted as a control group who received no training.

The interventions lasted one-and-a-half days, the stress management programmes were run by a team of Health

Authority clinical psychologists, the innovation training by a researcher from the Social and Applied Psychology Unit. Stress management training was similar in content to the programmes described earlier, whereas innovation training programmes attended to the causes and manifestations of strain at work and then introduced the concept of innovative coping. Participants, having identified work-related stressors, were encouraged to develop innovative responses through group discussion and individual action planning.

Participants completed self-report measures of psychological well-being (GHQ-12: Goldberg, 1972), job motivation and satisfaction (Warr, Cook & Wall, 1979), job-induced tension (House & Rizzo, 1972) and a measure of innovation. The results of the study indicated that both interventions were associated with improvements in psychological well-being. There were, however, interesting differences in the specific impacts of each intervention. After stress management training participants reported significantly lower psychological distress but no change in job-induced tension; after innovation training participants reported lower job-induced tension but no change in psychological distress. Because the GHQ is a measure of general well-being and the JIT is a more focused measure of work-related well-being this suggests that skills learned in stress management training are applied generally to a broad range of stressors (domestic as well as work-related) whereas skills from innovation training are more specifically applied to work problems. An additional difference between the two training groups was that benefits of stress management were more immediate whereas the benefits of innovation training were delayed.

At one year follow-up the effects of both interventions had diminished. Most outcome studies do not include such a long follow-up period and this finding suggests that all training courses should give attention to the maintenance of participants' new skills. In practice, this could be achieved by providing occasional booster sessions and by addressing the practical problems of implementing new skills in everyday life. Participants might also be encouraged to establish informal support networks where they could provide each other with support and practical advice.

The results of this study demonstrate that benefit is derived from both individually and organizationally focused stress management interventions. For the purpose of evaluation the distinction between the two training programmes was maximized. In practice a combination of both approaches may be most effective, whereby participants acquire skills which enable them to deal with their personal experiences and skills which enable them to identify and resolve some of the external job demands which hinder their effective performance and inhibit their well-being. In addition, in the present context, the interventions represent occupational strain reduction programmes (see Murphy, 1984) as participant groups were identified as experiencing above-average levels of occupational strain typical of health care workers (e.g. Firth, 1986; West & Rushton, 1986; Firth-Cozens & Morrison, 1987).

Research has yet to demonstrate whether similar benefits would derive from preventive programmes directed toward occupational groups under less strain. It is not known to what extent workers call upon learned skills when confronted with acute stress at work. Until more is known of the efficacy of preventive programmes the application of a 'needs diagnosis' (Ivancevich & Matteson, 1987), such as that described at the outset of the present chapter, is a worthwhile undertaking. This will help identify the carers who are most likely to benefit from stress management interventions.

CRITICAL INCIDENT DEBRIEFING

On 15 April 1989 a major accident occurred at Hillsborough Football Stadium in Sheffield. During the FA cup semi-final between Liverpool and Nottingham Forest 96 spectators were killed in a severe crush on the terraces and 159 casualties were subsequently treated by two major hospitals in Sheffield. One outcome of this tragedy was the acknowledgement locally that the psychological needs of staff in these hospitals, in dealing with this emergency and other potential emergencies, had previously never been fully considered. The personal experiences both of staff at the hospital sites in Sheffield and of workers involved in other tragic accidents and the emerging psychological literature together made it clear that indirect exposure to disasters and their aftermath often results in staff and others experiencing extreme emotional reactions. In the immediate aftermath of the Hillsborough tragedy, clinical psychologists from Sheffield and other local areas were directly involved in running debriefing sessions for Health Authority staff and other groups of employees whose work had brought them into contact with victims of the accident and their relatives.

The involvement of five psychologists from North Derbyshire had two immediate impacts. First was the acknowledgement that few clinicians had direct experiences of working in this context. Second, and more relevant in terms of planning, was the realization that within North Derbyshire there were no plans for dealing with the psychological effects of a similar disaster. A working group was formed with the primary task of coordinating the planning and development of services for staff, victims and relatives following a major disaster. This required the development of a complex network of resources that dovetailed with Local Authority plans and voluntary agencies.

Psychological Debriefing

The aim of psychological debriefing is to prevent longer term difficulties arising after exposure to a traumatic event that is outside the range of normal human experience and that would be markedly distressing to almost anyone. Extreme and distressing emotions are common after involvement in trauma and debriefing aims to normalize these emotions, to provide a framework for understanding them, and to enable staff to integrate their experiences and disengage themselves from them (Raphael, 1986). Debriefing is typically conducted with groups of staff soon after the impact of a disaster. The sessions are structured and contained. Usually they include an overview of possible emotional responses to disasters and the natural time course of these responses. Participants in the sessions are invited to describe how they became involved in the disaster and what they did during the crisis. Emotional experiences both during the acute phase of the crises and in the aftermath are discussed and the debriefing leaders will typically illustrate that individuals' emotional responses are varied and often idiosyncratic.

A team of 40 volunteers from within North Derbyshire Health Authority with counselling or mental health experience have been trained to lead debriefing sessions. Each is registered with the Occupational Health department and has been allocated to one of six teams. The organization of debriefers into teams enables each team to develop a cohesive structure, provides a convenient way of communicating with each volunteer and of updating training and enables each team to be coordinated through meetings between team leaders and the clinical psychologists who provide training and manage the service.

Major accidents on the scale of the Hillsborough Disaster are, thankfully, rare. However, health service staff are frequently exposed to smaller scale traumas such as road traffic accidents and other personal tragedies. These incidents can also be psychologically damaging to victims and carers and the psychological debriefing service is therefore available to individuals or groups on request. The large numbers of trained debriefers ensure that the service is easily and quickly accessible. The service also attempts to educate staff at all levels about the effects of traumatic experiences on psychological well-being so that it becomes an automatic and routine response to consider debriefing after any significant incident.

One aspect of this educational strategy has been the dissemination of information on debriefing through leaflets describing the purpose of debriefing and a booklet which details personal reactions to traumatic incidents. Psychologists from the coordinating group also meet with staff from Accident and Emergency, Intensive Care and other departments to discuss the effects of trauma and the way in which debriefing might be useful to them. The psychological impacts of traumatic incidents are not restricted to nursing, medical and paramedical staff. Other staff members such as ancillary staff, clerical and reception staff are often involved in distressing events and have direct contact with victims and their families.

ORGANIZATIONAL-LEVEL INTERVENTIONS

As the occupational stress work in NDHA has become more established and more widely known, opportunities for organizational-level interventions have arisen. These include requests from multidisciplinary teams for help with conflict resolution and establishing effective working relationships. Often these requests are initially presented as a need for stress management training courses for which the Psychology Department has now established a credible reputation. Other requests are for group or team development and yet others are concerned with contributing to management training in communication skills, motivation and leadership, or conflict resolution. In response to these varied requests and to the emerging consensus in the literature on occupational stress (Ganster et al., 1982; Murphy, 1988) a training and consultancy role has emerged for the Psychology Department.

The aim of this developing consultancy role is to integrate assessment of the presenting problems and levels of current distress, designing interventions through negotiation with managers and staff, facilitating the implementations of these interventions and evaluating their impact. Complementary activities include developing teaching and self-help materials and resources for use by managers, groups and individuals.

A recent case study illustrates the implementation of this organizational-level work and some of the difficulties that arise in formal evaluation of such interventions. The department agreed to work with two groups of community nurses (who were identified as in need of interventions by their managers) to resolve work- and team-related problems. The initial assessment was conducted using the Occupational Stress Indicator (OSI: Cooper, Sloan & Williams, 1988). The results of this assessment indicated that compared to other occupational groups, nurses in this sample scored significantly lower on job satisfaction and significantly higher on mental and physical ill health. Sources of job stress appeared to be relationships, organizational structure and climate, and the interface between home and work. These quantitative results were discussed with the community nurses and their managers, which helped to clarify more specific issues. Further meetings translated this information into collaborative action plans. Whilst these plans were different for each group, a consistent focus was on the interface between the nurses and the organization. This included increasing the amount of contact between managers and staff, sessions devoted to discussion of organizational change, presentation of a problem solving approach, and joint workshops for managers and staff aimed at enhancing mutual understanding and recognition of shared values.

The impact of these interventions was assessed after six months. Overall, the results of the intervention were mixed. Significant reductions were reported on the organizational structure and climate scales but none of the other scales were significantly different after the intervention. However, the impact of the interventions differed in the two groups. In one group, levels of physical and mental ill health were significantly improved as were levels of one subscale of job satisfaction. This finding suggests that the effects of the intervention were influenced by differences between the two groups.

A common feature of most models and theories of occupational stress is the assumption that the experience of stress arises from the interaction of an individual and their environment. Therefore, although intervening at an organizational level is a complex and difficult task, in principle it is a crucial component of a comprehensive approach to occupational stress interventions. Our experience suggests that it is important for managers and staff to share the responsibility of tackling work-related stress together. One focus of work, therefore, is the provision of assessment, advice and support to facilitate this joint responsibility. Encouragingly, requests for such assistance have increased as the result of informal publicity. There are therefore further opportunities to develop group-level intervention strategies in combination with the individually focused services already provided. Most importantly, these requests suggest that both staff and their managers are beginning to recognize their role in promoting their own psychological well-being at work.

CARING FOR THE CARERS: AN OVERVIEW

One of the initial tasks of the occupational stress initiative 'Caring for the Carers' within North Derbyshire Health Authority was the provision of recommendations to management which were described above. After seven years and continued organizational change, to what extent have these recommendations been followed? Clearly the Psychology Department, in collaboration with other departments, have been active in providing a wide, and increasing, range of services to staff. These services have been of undoubted benefit to individual employees and are increasingly supported by line managers. However, the focus of these services has predominantly been at an individual level. Most of the services are provided by the Psychology Department and other departments from within existing resources. Extra funding for the counselling service, the provision of stress management training or the development of organizational-level changes has not been provided from central resources so far, but is expected to be in the near future.

The reorganization of health services is a major source of uncertainty and anxiety for all staff. In addition to these negative consequences, continual changes mean that the continuity of management, the relationships between groups of professional health care staff, and the structure of the health service are all disrupted. Key personnel are moved to new management positions and managers themselves have a major task in keeping abreast of new policies and structures. The nature of health care work means that it is usually professional health care staff such as doctors, nurses and paramedical staff who are assumed to experience the greatest emotional difficulties at work and managers who should be working to minimize these demands. However, one of the barriers which managers face in implementing and supporting stress reduction strategies could be their own experience of uncertainty and role conflict in the face of cultural changes within the organization.

The achievements of the North Derbyshire Stress Working group are impressive, particularly when one notes that each individual member is him or herself subjected to many of the same organizational and work demands as experienced by health service staff. North Derbyshire Health Authority staff have established and supported a range of intervention strategies, each of which contributes to a slow but incremental change in organizational culture and attitudes. It is only by influencing this cultural change that the overall benefits of the 'Caring for the Carers' strategy will be seen. The promise of a psychologically healthy organization will become reality when all organization members accept their dual responsibility to contribute to the organizational goals and to the well-being of themselves and their colleagues.

REFERENCES

Beck, A. T. (1976). *Cognitive Therapy and the Emotional Disorders*. New York: International Universities Press.

Beer, M. & Walton, E. (1990). Developing the competitive organization: Interventions and strategies. *American Psychologist*, **45**, 154–161.

Berridge, J. & Cooper, C. L. (1993). Stress and coping in US organizations: The role of the Employee Assistance Programme. *Work & Stress*, **7**, 89–102.

Blair, A. (1992). Occupational stress among community nurses: Identification and intervention. Unpublished MSc thesis, University of Leicester.

Bruning, N. S. & Frew, D. R. (1987). Effects of exercise, relaxation and management skills training on physiological stress indicators: A field experiment. *Journal of Applied Psychology*, **72**, 515–521.

Bunce, D. J. & West, M. A. (1992). Stress management and innovation interventions at work. *SAPU Memo No. 1359*, University of Sheffield.

Cooper, C. L. & Mitchell, S. (1990). Nursing the critically ill and dying. *Human Relations*, **43**, 297–311.

Cooper, C. L., Sloan, S. J. & Williams, S. (1988). *Occupational Stress Indicator: Management Guide*. NFER-Nelson: Windsor.

DeFrank, R. S. & Cooper, C. L. (1987). Worksite stress management interventions: Their effectiveness and conceptualisation. *Journal of Managerial Psychology*, **2**, 4–10.

Firth, H. & Britton, P. (1989). Burnout, absence and turnover amongst British nursing staff. *Journal of Occupational Psychology*, **62**, 55–59.

Firth, J. A. (1986). Levels and sources of stress in medical students. *British Medical Journal*, **292**, 1177–1180.

Firth-Cozens, J. & Morrison, L. A. (1987). Sources of stress and ways of coping in junior house officers. *Stress Medicine*, **5**, 121–126.

Ganster, D. C., Mayes, B. T., Sime, W. E. & Tharp, G. D. (1982). Managing organisational stress: A field experiment. *Journal of Applied Psychology*, **67**, 533–542.

Goldberg, D. (1972). *The Detection of Psychiatric Illness by Questionnaire.* Oxford: Oxford University Press.

Handy, J. (1988). Theoretical and methodological problems within occupational stress and burnout research. *Human Relations*, **41**, 351–369.

House, R. J. & Rizzo, J. R. (1972). Towards the measurement of organizational practices: Scale development and validation. *Journal of Applied Psychology*, **56**, 388–396.

Hurrell, J. J. & Murphy, L. R. (1987). Stress management in the process of occupational stress reduction. *Journal of Managerial Psychology*, **2**, 18–23.

Ivancevich, J. M. & Matteson, L. M. (1987). Organizational level stress management interventions: A review and recommendations. *Journal of Organizational Behavioural Management*, **81**, 229–248.

Ivancevich, J. M., Matteson, M. T., Freedman, S. M. & Phillips, J. S. (1990). Worksite stress management interventions. *American Psychologist*, **45**, 252–261.

Jones, J. W., Barge, B. N., Steffy, B. D., Fay, L. M., Kunz, L. K. & Wuebker, L. J. (1988). Stress and medical malpractice: Organizational risk assessment and intervention. *Journal of Applied Psychology*, **73**, 727–735.

Kahn, R. L. & Byosiere, P. (1992). Stress in organizations. In M. D. Dunnette and L. M. Hough (eds), *Handbook of Industrial and Organizational Psychology*, vol. III. Palo Alto, CA: Consulting Psychologists Press.

Levitt, R. & Wall, A. (1992). *The Reorganized NHS.* London: Chapman & Hall.

Meichenbaum, D. (1985). *Stress Inoculation Training.* New York: Pergamon Press.

Murphy, L. R. (1984). Occupational stress management: A review and appraisal. *Journal of Occupational Psychology*, **57**, 1–15.

Murphy, L. R. (1988). Workplace interventions for stress reduction and prevention. In C. L. Cooper & R. Payne (eds), *Causes, Coping and Consequences of Stress at Work.* Chichester: Wiley.

Newman, J. E. & Beehr, T. A. (1979). Personal and organizational strategies for handling job stress: A review of research and opinion. *Personnel Psychology*, **32**, 1–43.

Nicholson, N. & West, M. A. (1988). *Managerial Job Change: Men and Women in Transition*. Cambridge: Cambridge University Press.

Parish, T. S. & Kappes, B. M. (1979). Affective implications of seeking psychological counselling. *Journal of Counselling Psychology*, **26**, 164–165.

Payne, R. & Firth-Cozens, J. A. (1987). *Stress in Health Professionals*. Chichester: Wiley.

Raphael, B. (1986). *When Disaster Strikes*. London: Hutchinson.

Rees, D. & Cooper, C. L. (1990). Occupational stress in health service workers in the U.K. *Stress Medicine*, **8**, 79–90.

Reynolds, S. A. & Shapiro, D. A. (1991). Stress reduction in transition: Conceptual problems in the design, implementation and evaluation of worksite stress management interventions. *Human Relations*, **44**, 717–733.

Reynolds, S. A., Taylor, E. & Shapiro, D. A. (1993). Session impact in stress management training. *Journal of Occupational and Organizational Psychology*, **66**, 99–113.

Reynolds, S. A., Taylor, E. & Shapiro, D. A. (in press). Session impact and outcome in stress management training. *Journal of Applied Social and Community Psychology*.

Sallis, J. F., Trevorrow, T. R., Johnson, C. C., Hovell, M. F. & Kaplan, R. M. (1987). Worksite stress management: A comparison of programmes. *Psychology and Health*, **1**, 237–255.

Sibicky, M. & Davido, J. F. (1986). Stigma of psychological therapy: Stereotypes, interpersonal reactions and the self-fulfilling prophecy. *Journal of Consulting and Clinical Psychology*, **33**, 148–154.

Swanson, N. G. & Murphy, L. R. (1991). Mental health counselling in industry. In C. L. Cooper & I. T. Robertson (eds), *International Review of Industrial and Organizational Psychology*, vol. 6. Chichester: Wiley.

Wall, T. D. & Clegg, C. W. (1981). Individual strain and organizational functioning. *British Journal of Clinical Psychology*, **20**, 135–136.

Warr, P. B., Cook, J., & Wall, T. D. (1979). Scales for the measurement of some work attitudes and aspects of psychological well-being. *Journal of Occupational Psychology*, **52**, 129–148.

West, M. A. (1989). Innovation amongst health care professionals. *Social Behaviour*, **4**, 173–184.

West, M. A. & Reynolds, S. (1993). Employee attitudes to work-based counselling services. Paper submitted for publication.
West, M. A. & Rushton, R. (1986). The drop-out factor. *Nursing Times/Nursing Mirror*, **52**, 29–31.

10
Gaining Control over the Work Environment

DOREEN M. MILLER
Former Chief Medical Officer of Marks & Spencer plc

INTRODUCTION

Marks and Spencer is an international retail organisation employing just over 50 000 people in the UK, of whom 83% are female and 66% are part-time. The company's aim is to provide quality merchandise representing good value for money. Customer service is a high priority at all times and two-thirds of staff in stores work on the sales floor to ensure the optimum standard of service to the customer.

The company's commitment to the well-being of its staff is well known. This is particularly evident in the development of policies and programmes which foster good human relations, fulfilling the needs of the individual and responding to the commercial objectives of the business. Training is viewed as important at all levels in the business to encourage individuals to take responsibility for improving their own skills. Emphasis is also placed on internal communication throughout the business, and all stores have communication groups whose terms of reference are regularly reviewed. Significantly, it was

Creating Healthy Work Organizations. Edited by C. L. Cooper and S. Williams.
© 1994 John Wiley & Sons Ltd

during a meeting between members of the Head Office Personnel Group and chairmen of store staff communication groups, that a statement was made to Health Services which was to mark a change in approach to problem solving in stores. 'Mental health is just as important as physical health', said a member of staff.

She went on to explain that, as a food sales assistant working at an electronic till point, she found the job provided little satisfaction and she felt undervalued. After thorough training for her till point job, she found that she had to maintain a fast work rate in order to obtain her performance-based bonus. In so doing, she did not have the time to provide the best service to customers at the end of each transaction by thanking them for their custom and exchanging a few words. In turn, the customers did not have the opportunity to speak to her and thank her, which would have helped her to feel valued.

The problem did not stop here. When technical problems occurred at the electronic till point, the sales assistant had to ring for help and, in so doing, lost ownership of the problem and its solution. The resultant feeling was that the computerised till point had changed the work environment and work practices. It had consequently left the sales assistant feeling as if she was an appendage to the machine with little control over the task. This inevitably had a negative impact on her performance and productivity, and in turn on the profitability of the business.

BACKGROUND TO THE PROJECT

The sales assistant had been perceptive in expressing the value placed on mental health at work. She was keen to improve her performance and wondered how she could do this.

The company's Occupational Health Service discussed the problem with a human resource consultancy specialising in continuous improvement programmes and the management of change. They agreed that the computerised till point had changed the workplace environment and created additional pressures on sales assistants which needed to be identified. At the same time, the commercial drive for increased throughput and the control of staffing levels was also adding to these pressures. Clearly, here was both a need and an opportunity to study the task of the food till sales assistant in detail, with a view to enhancing her mental well-being and performance. Benefits would consequently arise not only for staff members but also for their stores and the business as a whole.

All staff in Marks and Spencer are well trained for their job, and the existing staff involvement schemes such as the Suggestion Scheme and Communication Groups seemed to be the ideal forums through which the problems identified at food tills could be channelled. In consequence, it was considered that a programme run in conjunction with outside consultants, using their method of continuous improvement known as 'The Focus System', would be most productive.

The Focus System

The Focus System, which aimed to encourage every employee in a store to make an active ongoing contribution to the improvement in the business, was adopted to achieve this objective. It relied on a simple and easy to implement methodology with the following structure:

- Define the goal
- Find the constraints
- Make improvements
- Monitor the effects
- Share the results

The example already outlined had focused on a problem at food tills, and we had identified a consultancy we could work with to provide a methodology that could be applied to finding the solutions with the participation of all the staff. If this concept proved beneficial in a pilot study, the method could be adopted to resolve other problems arising from the store communication groups' findings, or—in a more proactive way—as a source of ideas for suggestion schemes in stores in the future.

It is important, however, to recognise that although the Focus System Group was separate from other staff involvement schemes, it was integrated with them to avoid confusion in the minds of staff. The Focus System provided a comprehensive methodology for involving employees at all levels in a structured and systematic group-based problem-solving activity. The employees' contributions were focused on very specific issues, which is the feature which gives the programme its distinctive power. The staff understood the issues and benefits to be gained from meeting the targets. By being responsible for their own performance, they would be committed to achieving success.

Responsibility and Ownership

This approach gave employees ownership of the problem, identifying that it was not a 'management problem' but 'their problem'. This is a very powerful emotion: people cannot solve others' problems for them. Staff will get things done if it is their responsibility to do so. When members of staff put their names on the board as members of the project team, they become associated with the issue. The system became identified as an employee-led and not a management-led project.

Team Development

People respond and give of their best when they work together. By creating a self-managed project team, members derived energy and support from their colleagues. However, in view of the new formation of the Focus Group, it was agreed that a junior member of the personnel management team should act as project coordinator. This role was one of 'facilitation and mentor' rather than manager. Senior management supported the Focus Group but did not get involved in the action.

The staff were enthusiastic and frequently gave up their own time to attend meetings on what to them was a staff project. The concept of the store-based improvement scheme was discussed with the director of store operations, Central Personnel and Health Services. The idea was welcomed and it was agreed that a pilot study would take place in the Marble Arch and Leeds stores. Here was an opportunity to enhance the performance of staff through them gaining greater control of the job, as well as more responsibility for decision-making and solving problems. It promised to heighten individuals' feeling of being valued and, in addition, to provide commercial benefits through greater productivity and better customer service.

The interest shown in stores was reflected in Head Office by this remark from the store Operations Director:

> If, by encouraging staff to take more responsibility for solving their own problems, this results in improved morale through having more control over their work and improved productivity at tills results, I'm all for it. If the study demonstrates that staff can contribute to improving performance and, by involving them in an ongoing improvement programme, their self-esteem and job satisfaction increases resulting in improved profitability, that's great. If you can develop it into a structured, systematic, self-sufficient and sustainable programme, lets go for it!

Action Plan Objective and Method

The *project objective* was defined as being:

To develop a programme that would raise the self-esteem and job satisfaction of employees by involving them in work-based problem-solving groups.

The *method* required a pilot study to be set up for the Marble Arch and Leeds stores. The study would be planned as one which was designed to achieve a measurable improvement in performance, as well as an understanding of the process in each store, rather than as a training exercise.

The project comprised three preliminary phases:

1 Selection of a project leader for each store.
2 Composition of groups in the pilot stores: e.g.

- Junior management group
- Food sales assistant group
- General merchandise sales assistant group
- Non-management mixed group
- Multistore group

3 Key topics for participant briefing programme:

- Background to the project
- Theory of constraints and the throughput world
- Work-based, problem-solving techniques
- Practical exercise in identifying the topics for analysis
- Action plan
- Work group sessions
- Monitoring, evaluation and improvement of the performance of the groups using the above techniques
- Development of the improvement plan
- Implementation plan

The project leader was guided in the choice of topics which were clearly definable, measurable and understandable. The group had their own ideas on the most critical improvement targets and the following examples illustrate the improvements set for Marble Arch store:

- To reduce the delays through till stoppages by 20%
- To improve average throughput by 15%
- To reduce stock levels by 10% in 3 months without affecting performance
- To reduce shelf filling time by 10% without overstocking
- To reduce chilled food wastage by 10%

Each of the goals was geared to achieving a financial benefit but did not involve capital expenditure. The stores undertaking the pilot studies were challenged by being asked to achieve improvements which contributed towards the company's performance. The programme emphasised the quantity as well as the quality of improvements and, in the early stages, it proved helpful to set the groups a target of 100 implemented improvements to be achieved within 3 months.

During the pilot study, the consultant's role was to facilitate the process to enable the stores to develop their own store-based improvement system which would become self-sufficient within 6 months. The project was started in January 1992 and the results were to be reviewed at the end of April.

THE MARBLE ARCH STORE PROJECT— ELECTRONIC TILL POINT OPERATIONS

Background

In Marks and Spencer stores, the Food Department is a sizeable and complex operation. High levels of throughput, contained within a framework of offering the customer a high quality product in a fast, efficient and courteous manner, require a variety of both personal and technical skills from the sales assistants.

Within the Food Department, the till point operation is regarded as the least attractive part of a sales assistant's role. Confined within a narrow space and seated well below the average height of customers, dealing with a constant stream of shoppers in a noisy environment for up to four hours at a time had ensured that it was an activity to be avoided.

It was not surprising, therefore, that this activity was chosen to form the basis of a Store-Based Improvement Study. The opportunity to take part in a pilot scheme involving general sales assistants in reviewing an everyday operation and making recommendations for improvement was immediately well received.

Initial Briefing

This included an explanation of the concept of store-based improvement and an outline of the implementation process. Project selection was left to the store. However, there was encouragement to focus on an issue that would represent a challenge and produce improvements which would ultimately contribute to the store's overall performance.

Initially, the management team were asked to nominate a small number of staff members who would form the project team. A mix of abilities, interests and areas of responsibility was considered desirable. In addition, a member of the management team was selected to be responsible for running the project and assisting in the briefing of the team members.

Implementation

The first stage of the project was to bring the team together to familiarise them with the concept and method of the programme. The session was attended by the consultant and was designed to be participative, practical and interactive. Particular activities included brain-storming, team working, problem identification and solving, and also the introduction and use of the focus chart.

The focus chart was a central part of the project in terms of maintaining attention to the topic, recording initiatives, reviews and recommendations, and focusing the effort towards achieving the goal.

The team members were then asked to confirm the specific objectives and left to meet again on their own to determine how to publicise and launch the project within the store.

The specific project objectives chosen by the Marble Arch team were concerned with:

- Ensuring all staff spend an equal period of time operating the food till
- Ensuring that no member of staff spent more than three hours on a till at any one time

These objectives were seen to be those considered most desirable by the majority of the food sales staff.

By reducing the time spent on the till to three hours from the existing level of four or more hours, and ensuring equal rotation, it was believed that all staff would be more willing to perform their share of the duty. In addition, a reduction in the time spent on the till would reduce the problems of fatigue, stress and aches and pains, resulting in the staff being fresher and more positive in their customer contact. Importantly, it was recognised that achievement of the objectives would lead to increased job satisfaction and self-esteem by the food sales assistants and help in achieving increased productivity and performance.

The Marble Arch team consisted of four staff members, and an Assistant Personnel Manager. They decided to promote the project by setting the Focus Chart in a main part of the Staff Lounge area and to man the stand during coffee and lunch breaks. Staff were asked to make recommendations on how to achieve the two main objectives. No restrictions were placed on the number of suggestions made, or on their viability. The project team then collated all the ideas and compiled them together in a log book. A number of issues were raised which not only concerned the key objectives but related to the operation at the till point, the layout and design of equipment, attitudes of other staff members, and Customer Service. Problems associated with ergonomic features of the existing till point design were addressed before the project started.

A particularly successful by-product of the project concerned the future design of till points. As an outcome of the energy and enthusiasm of the project team, a representative visited the till point manufacturers with members of the Head Office buying team to give the 'user' view on a prototype design which had been trialled in their store.

Evaluating the Process

The project ran for a monitored period of six weeks. The momentum to sustain effort and achieve the objectives was maintained throughout by all team members of the food staff. The two key objectives were met and, using the recommendations gleaned through the process, were speedily implemented with total support.

Equally valuable was the benefit to both staff members and management arising from the positive effects of the programme itself. In the case of staff members, they gained particularly from:

- Recognition
- A feeling of being valued and enhanced self-esteem
- Involvement and participation
- Improved problem recognition and solving skills
- Enhanced communication skills
- Ability to influence upwards
- Greater integration with other parts of the store
- Increased job satisfaction

In addition, the project leader who was an Assistant Personnel Manager also gained through:

- A deeper understanding of staff needs
- Recognition of staff ability to identify problems and present solutions
- Confidence to manage 'remotely'
- Development of further motivational skills
- Sense of achievement and completion

The store also gained a wider benefit from the process as it was then better equipped to translate ideas into solutions when faced with the everyday operational problems that arise.

Lessons Learnt

Having applied the process, achieved the objective and recognised the value of the process for use in further in-store exercises, lessons were learnt on how to further improve the concept.

It was appreciated that a highly motivated, enthusiastic and committed member of the management team was needed to drive the programme when necessary. The skill of this individual, however, would be seen as being able to motivate and inspire without dominating and applying too much management control. The staff members should feel confidence from receiving guidance and support but still retain a clear awareness that they were 'in the driving seat'.

Whilst the size of the team can be flexible, an optimum number would be between 6 and 10. This ensures that there can be division of workload without overburdening, and that there is sufficient personality mix to generate and maintain momentum. The team should be encouraged throughout the process by reward for achievement. The example of a member of the team, a sales assistant, visiting a till point supplier with the Head Office buying team demonstrated the value of giving recognition to her ability to contribute.

Summary

The project provided an opportunity to evaluate, through practical use, the Store-Based Improvement Study. It clearly succeeded in confirming that by involving staff members at all levels in evaluating issues and processes, as well as identifying problems and making recommendations in the scope of their everyday duties, it provided a wide range of benefits. These were felt collectively by the staff members, management and the store in general as morale was boosted, involvement and integration developed and problems were resolved jointly— and with a high degree of ownership.

THE LEEDS STORE PROJECT—THEFT AND LOSS REDUCTION

Background

In discussion with our consultant, the Leeds store decided to develop a programme aimed at raising the self-esteem and job satisfaction of employees by involving them in work-based problem solving.

The objectives set by the store were to:

1 Establish a Focus Group and identify the subject matter.
2 Develop a mechanism which allowed staff to help solve current problems by finding their own solutions.
3 Ensure that all staff were given the opportunity to contribute to improving performance by involving them in an ongoing programme which would increase their self-esteem and job satisfaction as well as having a positive impact on profitability.

Project selected: 'To reduce the theft and loss levels in the store'. *The project team of 12* comprised sales, operations, and administration assistants, deputy and full-time supervisors, and the store secretary. The message to everyone was that the method to be used was one of 'total participation for all'. *The Target*: To reduce the store loss per week by 20% before the next stocktake.

The Method

A poster in the shape of a fish skeleton was placed on the notice board, for use as the focal point for all activities. The Project Group launched the project during a lunch period by offering all participants a glass of Bucks Fizz and a piece of cake. Staff were encouraged to make observations, suggest improvements or come up with ideas which were noted on the post-it stickers and attached to the 'fish bones'. It was the duty of the Group to discuss the observations, improvements and ideas that emerged, providing feedback to all individual contributors and testing suggestions where appropriate. No suggestion was deemed too trivial to warrant personal discussion.

About one fifth of the overall store personnel, 75 people, contributed with observations, ideas and improvements to reducing the loss, resulting in the following tally:

- 35 observations
- 12 improvements
- 28 ideas

Initially, many of the observations were of a minor nature but as more people became involved, real problems came to the surface which warranted investigation.

The Focus Group monitored and evaluated areas of shrinkage that could be significantly reduced by members of staff taking greater care when dealing with the company's assets. All such findings were notified to members of staff on eye-catching posters or news-sheets. At the same time, the Supervision team in the store was separately involved in working to combat theft and loss. Although methods were different, ideas and suggestions were interchanged and cooperation between the two groups was excellent.

Arising from the Focus Group's work, a number of issues causing concern, together with remedial action, were highlighted through the 'post-it note' system. Examples included:

1 *Undamaged stock was constantly being thrown out as rubbish* and returned to the distribution centre. Reliance was put on their goodwill to return this stock to the store—*but* at a cost!

Action: Staff were made responsible for separating plastic and card before returning trolleys emptied of stock to the warehouse. Operations staff took responsibility for monitoring rubbish and returned all recovered stock to a central display point as a means of highlighting to all staff members what stock was being lost, as well as 'how' and 'when'.

2 *It was easy for thieves to steal high-priced merchandise.*
   Action: Staff now inform security of the location of expensive goods to ensure that this merchandise is in full view of the CCTV camera.

3 *Food was being consumed as customers shopped before it was purchased.*
   Action: Tickets have been printed asking customers not to consume food before it has been paid for.

4 *Till errors were above an acceptable level; errors in till counting occurred.*
   Action: Selective tills were counted manually; retraining sessions were given to all concerned and, subject to a few exceptions, till counts improved. A trial of counting £1 coins instead of weighing them resulted in discrepancies being discovered: new weighing scales were consequently purchased.

5 *The loading bay was vulnerable during deliveries.*
   Action: Bolts were fitted to the loading doors and holes drilled into the asphalt, enabling the gates to be closed up to the side of the vehicle and thereby avoiding illicit access.

6 *Contractors' vehicles were not included in the routine bag and contractor searches.*
   Action: The vehicles have been included in the early morning and late night audit checks.

7 *Uncertainty that all goods listed on the delivery notes were being received.*
   Action: Resulting from a 100% delivery check on one department, a small discrepancy was found. Random 100% checks are now carried out on deliveries.

8   *Internal theft—(this was a major concern of all staff).*
     Action: The Focus Team requested that the Supervision
     Team undertake this task. Checks are now carried out at
     various times of the day with the full approval of all staff.

9   *Till procedures not being followed at all times.*
     Action: A 'Do you know' bulletin itemising the correct till
     procedure was circulated in the dining room for all
     members of staff to read (see Appendix 10.1).

10   *Lack of recording of known losses.*
     Action: A bulletin was produced to highlight the
     importance of recording these data (see Appendix 10.2).

In addition to these initial actions, the Focus Group
continued to investigate other ideas which could result in
further reductions in theft and loss. For example:

1   Induction training to focus on theft and loss as key issues of
    concern.
2   Ensuring that testers are always available for cosmetics to
    avoid soiled and damaged goods.
3   Improving the security access to backstage areas.
4   Improving the accuracy in completing administrative
    documents.
5   Preventing 'price swapping': e.g. switching higher priced
    brassieres into lower priced packaging; switching adhesive
    bar codes.
6   Theft in lifts: (warning notices were subsequently displayed
    in lifts as a deterrent).

To gain first-hand experience in preventive measures for shop
theft and irregular till procedures, the Focus Team manned the
store's CCTV equipment for periods.

Results

The Focus Team had set themselves a *target to reduce the store loss by 20% before the next stocktaking.* After eight weeks, the results were as follows:

- The loss per week had been reduced from over 2% in spring 1992 to 1.36% at the first stocktaking after the launch. This figure continued to drop at subsequent stocktakes.

Comment

The work of the Focus Group within the store was successful in achieving its objective: an additional benefit was the considerable involvement of all members of the group in this exercise. Whilst requiring the involvement and guidance of management initially, they soon started to introduce initiatives and effect changes themselves. Thereafter, management merely had to be kept informed.

Leeds store has recently used the Focus Group method for its Communication Group activities. As a result, the Communication Group is taking responsibility for solving its own problems and is less dependent on Senior Management and Head Office.

The benefits of giving staff ownership of problems and the opportunity to solve them themselves had a direct and visible effect on their feelings, particularly of being valued and contributing to the success of the store's profitability.

FOLLOW-UP

The report arising from the Focus Group exercise in Marble Arch and Leeds stores was sent to all UK stores explaining how these groups had successfully identified and solved problems.

Six months later, this work influenced new developments in the stores which had undertaken the pilot study. Till work had previously involved high physical demands with low decision-making, creating pressures for staff which they had no opportunity to change. This activity is now regarded by all staff as a key part of the job, while they recognise too that the length of time they are required to perform this function is limited. In consequence, they are satisfied with the work as they are now making decisions and feel that responsibility and control have been placed on them. The successful outcome of the exercise has also resulted in tangible, cost-saving benefits with the abolition of till controllers and the faster throughput of goods. The net result is improved customer service, more efficient work practices and—most important—more effective and contented staff.

Staff continue to contribute new ideas and have applied the same problem-solving technique to other situations, providing solutions without having to refer to Senior Management or Head Office. All stores have now been asked to consider if the formation of a Focus Group in their store might help staff to address and solve problems with the resultant benefits that have already been demonstrated.

ACKNOWLEDGEMENTS

The author wishes to thank the management and staff of Marks & Spencer's Marble Arch, London, and Leeds stores for their valuable contribution of case history information.

APPENDIX 10.1

DO YOU KNOW?

News Letter No. 1

1. You should not serve relatives, friends or other members of staff without first calling a Supervisor or Controller to witness the transaction. The transaction should be witnessed from start to finish.

2. All transactions using staff discount vouchers MUST be witnessed by a Supervisor or Controller—even those from other stores.

3. Size of merchandise (not size on hanger) should be repeated to the customer.

4. All over rings MUST be claimed for—call a Supervisor or Controller.

5. Amount of money tendered by the customer should be repeated to the customer.

6. Change MUST be counted out into the customer's hand. (This provides a second check that the correct change is being tendered.)

7. All cheque cards MUST be scrutinised thoroughly prior to acceptance—signature, date, sort code on card must correspond with those on the cheque.

8. You MUST give the customer your full attention at all times.

LEEDS STORE : FOCUS GROUP

APPENDIX 10.2

ARE YOU RECORDING
KNOWN LOSSES?

News Letter No. 2

Your Textile Supervisor carries a card to record:
Testers
Soiled and Damaged:
Dresses without belts
Items used for promotion which have become soiled
Items with broken packages which cannot be used as testers
Cost of odd shoes
Ceramics broken on display
Spot reductions
Your Food Supervisors have a sheet to record:
Food consumed by a tasting panel
Food used on display which cannot be put back into stock

The above list represents a sample of KNOWN LOSSES

If they are not recorded they become UNKNOWN LOSSES

Please make sure your Supervisor records all the above.
It is everybody's responsibility to ensure this is done.

LEEDS STORE : FOCUS GROUP

11
The Role of Employee Assistance Programmes

CHULY LEE
JEFFREY A. GRAY
Institute of Psychiatry, London

INTRODUCTION

What Are Employee Assistance Programmes?

The term 'employees assistance programme' was originally introduced by the National Institute of Abuse and Alcoholism (NIAAA) in the United States during World War II to describe their occupational alcoholism programme. It was hoped that this term would render the service more acceptable (Sonnenstuhl and Trice, 1986). The employee assistance, or counselling programme (EAP), as we know it today, is largely a product of the 1960s: it now usually offers assistance to workers with personal problems of a more general nature, as well as problems related specifically to alcohol abuse.

Today, EAPs have diversified into a range of systems, comprising different sponsorships, structures, processes, target populations, names and even objectives. Nonetheless, despite this diversity, there is general agreement on what

Creating Healthy Work Organizations. Edited by C. L. Cooper and S. Williams.
© 1994 John Wiley & Sons Ltd

constitutes an EAP. In the United States the Employee Assistance Professionals Association (EAPA) provides the following definition:

> An employee assistance program (EAP) is a worksite-based program designed to assist in the identification and resolution of productivity problems associated with employees impaired by personal concerns including, but not limited to: health, marital, family, financial, alcohol, drug, legal, emotional, stress, or other personal concerns which may adversely affect employee job performance. The specific core activities of EAPs include (1) expert consultation and training to appropriate persons in the identification and resolution of job performance issues..., and (2) confidential, appropriate and timely problem-assessment services, referrals...treatment and assistance...and formation of linkages between workplace and community resources that provide such services... (EAPA, 1990)

Thus, underlying the diversity of terms and organizational structures that constitute an EAP programme, the ultimate concern is with *preventing*, *identifying*, and *treating* personal problems that adversely affect job performance.

Historical Development of EAPs

By the end of the nineteenth century, sporadic efforts were being made by workers and unions to improve social welfare services in the United States. During this period, management and unions alike began to integrate humanitarian values with economic concerns, and to consider the possibility that helping workers with their personal problems might contribute to increased productivity (Brandes, 1970). With the movement towards social betterment came inexpensive housing, company-sponsored unions, better working environments, medical care and education. However, during the mid-1920s this movement started to lose its momentum. The reasons for this change, as suggested by Brandes (1970), included the economic depression, the Wagner Act of 1936 outlawing company-sponsored unions and, on the part of workers, increasing opposition to the paternalistic attitude of their employers. These factors forced many companies to cut back on services, and discouraged the provision of comprehensive welfare programmes. Thus it was not until the 1940s that the next wave of development in social services for workers took place.

The first important contribution lay in the occupational alcoholism movement. Historically, the chief predecessors of the EAP were occupational alcoholism programmes started during World War II, and based on the principles of Alcoholics Anonymous (AA). For example, in the early 1940s, the medical departments at Du Pont de Nemours and Eastman Kodak Company established two of the first alcohol programmes in the workplace, with many other companies following suit by the late 1940s (McGowan, 1984). During this period, an increase in the activity of groups of concerned individuals, combined with government recognition, contributed to a heightened awareness of alcohol-related issues in the workplace. By the mid-1950s, there were approximately 50 to 60 industrial alcoholism programmes in the United States (Trice and Schonbrunn, 1981).

The National Council on Alcoholism, the Occupational Program Consultants Association, the NIAAA, and the American Federation of Labor and Congress of Industrial Organizations (AFL–CIO) are some of the national groups that emerged during this period; they advocated the development of broad-based programmes to assist alcoholic workers and to train professionals in this area. By the 1970s, industrial programmes came to play an integral role in the identification and treatment of alcoholics; and with the establishment of the NIAAA in 1971, an organization was for the first time set up to market occupational programmes to business. This new development of diverse programmes at a national level reflected new insights: the importance of training supervisors to enable them (i) to make referrals, rather than just diagnosing alcoholism, and (ii) to provide assistance for a wider range of behavioural–medical problems (McGowan, 1984).

A second important contribution lay in the development of the various mental health professions, such as psychology, psychiatry, and counselling. The first model of personnel counselling grew out of the work of Elton Mayo (1923) and experiments conducted at Western Electric by Roethlisberger and Dickson in the 1930s. These researchers recommended that companies should manage workers' irrational emotions by paying more attention to their feelings and concerns, and that workers should be encouraged to express their feelings and to work through their problems rationally. Throughout the 1940s and 50s, Western Electric's programme played an important role in the establishment of counselling programmes for personnel in other plants. Although management was far from providing massive support for research of this kind, these influential early studies sparked an interest in occupational mental health, and researchers began to focus on the relationship between mental health and work (Presnall, 1981).

A third contributing factor was the labour unions' support of social service programmes for their members. Historically, the unions preferred to operate their own health programmes, and indeed they offered a wide range of services. The National Maritime Union and United Seamen's Service, started in 1943, is one of the better known programmes, while the United Mine Workers Health Services similarly set up a short-term mental health programme in 1948. Other union counselling programmes were also initiated during World War II, and continue today under the auspices of the AFL–CIO as the oldest EAP in the United States.

Although occupational mental health programmes and new social services were introduced gradually in the 1950s and the 1960s, the real breakthrough in employee counselling did not take place until well into the 1970s. As mentioned earlier, the establishment of the NIAAA in 1971 was a significant turning point, as various groups concerned with workers' welfare converged on a common interest—that of helping workers with their personal problems. Since that time, a combination of humanitarian concern for the good treatment of workers and economic concern for their productivity has continued to influence the development of EAPs, though the balance between these two concerns has not always been equal. Past research and experience have helped to shape the essential belief that EAPs serve both business and labour to achieve productivity and to preserve human capital by offering a unified approach to intervention and assistance for a variety of personal problems in and out of the workplace.

Evidence of the growing support for EAPs, as more employers realize the need for this kind of assistance in pursuing productivity objectives, is provided by the US Department of Labor (1990), which reported that 78.8% of large employers (250 employees or more) had EAPs in 1990 compared to 51.3% in 1988.

Among medium-sized employers, EAP utilization rates rose from 19.3 to 39.3% during the same period (EAPA, 1992a). An increasing number of employers now take the initiative in offering EAPs so as to improve relations with their workforce. A further influential factor lies in US federal regulations: since 1986, federal agencies have been required to provide EAP services for their employees, and many state and local governments are beginning to follow suit.

EAP PROGRAMME COMPONENTS

In this section we review in more detail the essential components of an EAP, and the decisions that need to be taken in setting one up. Because EAPs vary along so many dimensions, it is difficult simply to categorize programme options or models. There are, however, some key issues that must be considered prior to and during the implementation of an EAP. There is no clear logical order in which these issues should be addressed; they are all, however, important. In approaching them, three general questions should be borne in mind: (i) What is covered in the programme? (ii) Who accomplishes the functions that make it up? (iii) How are they to be accomplished?

Erfurt and Foote (1985) grouped variations in EAP functions into three general areas: (i) case finding or the identification of employees who need or want assistance; (ii) the source of the EAP service; and (iii) the types of services available to employees. Figure 11.1 illustrates the points at which variations in EAPs can take place.

EAP Objectives

Clarification of the basic objectives of the programme, and of the general policies it is meant to serve, is essential. In this connection, questions that need to be addressed by the

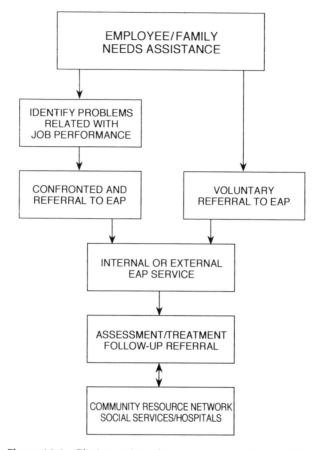

Figure 11.1   *Choice points determining variations in EAPs*

commissioning organization include the following:

1   What is the core mission of the EAP?
2   Who is eligible for its services?
3   What types of problems will be handled?
4   What is the role of the employee?
5   What are the roles of: line management? trade unions? occupational health services? personnel officers?
6   What is the route of referral?

General guidelines to EAP objectives are provided by the EAP Professional Program Standards (EAPA, 1990, as follows:

1   To serve the organization, its employees, and their families, by providing a comprehensive system from which

employees can obtain assistance in addressing personal problems which may affect their work performance.

2 To serve as a resource for management and labor when they intervene with employees whose personal problems affect job performance.

3 To effectively, efficiently, and professionally provide assessment, referral, and follow-up services for mental health, alcohol, and other drug-related problems in the workforce.

It is evident from the history of the development of EAPs that individual programmes vary widely in their specific objectives, depending on their origin. Many of the early programmes developed as a means to deal with alcohol-related problems. These focused specifically on alcoholism, and the programme was handled by experienced or interested lay persons within the organization (Trice and Schonbrunn, 1981). The focus of other programmes has lain in counselling employees in relation to a wider range of problems; these have tended to be operated by professionals, such as psychologists or counsellors. In many cases, the initial objectives of a programme are determined by the particular individuals within the company who establish it—often a committed person or group—and by the reasons they have for wishing to do so.

The objectives of the programme are often of the greatest importance in accounting for its design, as they influence which activities are included, what kind of staffing arrangement is required, and the distribution of activities within the commissioning organization and/or external provider. For example, programmes operated by recovering alcoholics with help from an outside voluntary organization, such as the AA, often adopt a self-help and informal structure. Programmes emphasizing counselling by professionals, on the other hand, usually take on a more formal structure within the company. If, as a further example, the primary objective of an EAP is to reduce absenteeism, then the programme design can be expected to stress (i) methods for identifying and confronting workers who present this problem, and (ii) monitoring and follow-up of such workers within the company. However, if a central programme objective is to provide services to as many employees as possible, then the identification of cases will be emphasized without follow-up by the company (Erfurt and Foote, 1985).

Programme Models

The next step is to determine what EAP model is to be implemented. The choice of a particular programme model should reflect the resources available to the organization, the needs of its employees, and the size of the organization. The various existing models have been grouped into the following three general types by Jones (1985).

Full-Service Programmes

These have the following characteristics:

- comprehensive services
- available to employees and dependents
- available to retirees and dependents
- available to disabled and dependents
- any kind of problem
- unlimited usage
- no cost to user
- 24 hours per day, seven days per week
- live answering service and/or pager
- voluntary
- confidential
- service provided by professional clinicians
- follow-up service provided
- outreach service available
- supervisory training provided
- orientation provided to employees
- onwards referrals made

Cooper, Sadri, Allison and Reynolds (1990) suggest that the most effective way to manage stress is to intervene at all three of the following levels: (i) the individual (e.g. via relaxation, behavioural and cognitive therapy, etc.); (ii) the individual/organizational interface (e.g. relationships at work, work role);

and (iii) the organization (e.g. structure, training, selection, physical environment). A comprehensive stress management programme should aim at all three levels, since stress can be caused by both work-related and personal events. However, even a full-service EAP aims only at the first of these levels. A fully comprehensive company policy to deal with all stress and stress-related issues needs also to address problems at the other two levels. However, to do so within the framework of the EAP itself risks compromising clinical confidentiality (see below, Issues in EAP Management).

Limited Utilization Programmes

- approximately 5–8 free sessions provided and services charged beyond this
- fee for service arrangement

Information and Referral Only Programmes

- no individual counselling sessions
- referrals made by telephone
- little or no follow-up

EAP Service Delivery Systems

Another critical decision is to determine the delivery model: by an internal or external provider, or as a combined programme. An internal programme is delivered by professionals or non-professionals employed by the company; an external programme is delivered by EAP professionals under contract to the company. In reaching this decision, it is essential that the company has a clear grasp of what it, as an organization, is capable of delivering.

In-House or Internal Services

In-house services can range from the simple giving of information to extensive face-to-face psychotherapeutic treatment. These programmes are generally conducted by internal staff with professional training, for example psychologists, physicians, social workers, occupational health nurses, or specialists such as alcoholism counsellors. However, the internal staff may at times have only limited training or have a personal interest in relevant problems, for example recovered alcoholics or drug-abusers, medical department staff other than physicians. Whenever possible, an internal EAP is probably best placed under the direction of the medical department, due to the nature of the problems that are assessed and treated. These may be psychological, behavioural, marital, family-related, or concerned with substance abuse. Dealing with them is likely to require expert knowledge and skills in the fields of psychology, counselling, use of tests, and assessment procedures. Staff competence is obviously critical in ensuring that proper care is provided.

Large companies (2000 or more employees) generally have an in-house Occupational Health Department staffed by professionals of several kinds, while smaller companies tend to favour external resources. Thus, the size of the organization is closely related to the choice of the EAP delivery system. Companies develop in-house programmes for various reasons, for example because they are considered to be cost-effective or believed to be the most suitable way to express the company's concerns to its employees (Sonnenstuhl and Trice, 1986).

External Services

External service delivery can be operated by a single agency or by a consortium of firms that jointly provide an EAP. Services of this kind are delivered by groups of EAP professionals, who liaise with an internal department or person responsible for coordinating and monitoring the programme. The staffing of an external service will vary according to the type of programme and the scope of services provided. These may include a variety of options besides assessment and treatment, such as supervisor training, special workshops, programme evaluation, or appropriate referrals to other agencies. It is usually the employee who initiates contact with the external service. For this purpose, the external service provider often operates a 'hot' telephone line that employees can use to gain immediate access to the service network.

Many companies make external arrangements because it gives them increased flexibility: an external provider can provide a greater and more differentiated range of resources; their existing service package is quicker to implement, for example in response to a sudden increase in critical incidents; the programme can also be discontinued more readily, since the company does not take on additional staff of its own; elimination of the need for additional staff also reduces overhead costs; and the company can save time for existing medical or personnel staff by delegating the responsibility of coordinating the programme to the external provider.

EMPLOYEE ASSISTANCE PROGRAMMES IN THE UK

Despite the dramatic expansion in the implementation of EAPs in the United States, this type of employee service has received relatively little attention in the UK, where it was not introduced until the late 1980s. It is only recently that UK companies have begun to adopt a systematic approach to the management and development of their human resources, and to realize the enormous potential benefits that may come from doing this well. The tougher economic climate, a growing disillusion with the National Health Service, and increasing recognition of the effects of stress on performance are just some of the factors which have contributed to making UK employers examine new strategies for maintaining performance and productivity. A small but nonetheless significant number of employers are beginning to incorporate counselling in the workplace as part of their general employee benefit schemes.

The Confederation of British Industry (1993) recently published the results of a survey to illustrate the significance of absenteeism in the workplace and the ramifications of its effects, both direct and indirect, on productivity. The causes of absenteeism were ranked in the following order by respondents to the survey: (i) work-related stress; (ii) poor motivation; (iii) family responsibilities, (iv) low priority given to absence control; (v) job insecurity, (vi) drink or drug-related problems; and (vii) unauthorized extension of holidays. Respondents were asked to select factors which would help reduce absenteeism, and they rated management commitment and improved monitoring as the two top factors. The same report estimated that sickness absenteeism cost UK business £13 billion in 1992. Reports such as this lead companies to recognize the need for organizational changes so as to improve performance, and they emphasize the value of providing comprehensive counselling services for employees and their families. In response to this growing public awareness and acceptance of support services for employees, EAP programmes are now available in many forms. A full-service external EAP developed in the UK will be illustrated in the following section.

Exhibit Case: The StressCare Programme

The StressCare EAP is an example of a 'full-service programme' as distinguished by Jones (1985) (see above). Highly flexible and comprehensive, it has been developed jointly by two external providers, CareAssist (a subsidiary of Royal Insurance) and Psychology at Work (an initiative of the Department of Psychology at the Institute of Psychiatry, London University, attached to the Maudsley Hospital). The programme offers counselling across the full range of psychological, inter-personal, emotional and stress-related problems, including those related to marital, family, alcohol or substance abuse or work issues. As well as psychological counselling, it provides legal advice, debt counselling and advice on consumer problems. The programme is staffed by qualified clinical psychologists, counsellors, and lawyers who assist employees and/or their families as appropriate, depending on the nature of the problem.

As in many EAPs, the employee accesses all the programme's constituent services through a single telephone number, the call then being directed to an appropriate counsellor. No information other than the caller's company scheme number is required, giving the caller the opportunity to maintain complete anonymity if so desired. The telephone counselling service is staffed 24 hours a day, 365 days a year, by both counsellors and lawyers. Once the caller—who can be the employee or a family member—makes contact with the service, immediate assessment and counselling is offered. The caller has unlimited access to the telephone counselling service, and can speak to the same counsellor each time. If, as is often the case, there is a mix of legal and emotional problems (e.g. in connection with divorce proceedings), transfer is made between psychological and legal counselling as needed.

If, in the clinical judgement of the counsellor or at the request of the client, the case would benefit from face-to-face counselling, the counsellor arranges an appointment with a clinical psychologist or a specialist counsellor in the area where the caller lives or works. For this purpose, the telephone counsellors are able at once to access a nationwide network of psychologists and other counsellors who are accredited to the programme. Depending on the particular contractual arrangements with the commissioning company, a limit (typically, eight) is set on the number of face-to-face sessions per employee per annum. Although this limit is set partly to control costs, it also has a clinical basis. It is known both from reports of clinical trials and from experience with the programme that many of the problems typically encountered will respond rapidly to appropriate treatment and counselling. Often, three to four sessions are enough, especially if backed up by the client's own 'homework'; if no improvement is obtained within about eight to ten sessions, it is likely that further treatment will continue to be ineffective (Marks, 1987). If the problem is one that is unsuitable for psychological treatment or is not resolved within the limit of eight sessions, onward referrals are made as appropriate in the private sector or in the NHS. For example, a client with a depression that fails to respond to cognitive/behavioural therapy (Hackman, 1993) would probably be referred to a psychiatrist for drug treatment; though it should be noted that the success of pharmacological and psychological treatments, respectively, for depression is about equal (Dobson, 1989). At the termination of the face-to-face sessions, the client can contact the telephone counsellor for continued unlimited support.

To maximize the effectiveness of the StressCare programme once it is implemented, additional back-up services are provided, such as workshops for staff in occupational medicine, personnel or line management, as well as employees generally; or training in dealing with problems likely to arise in the particular industry concerned—for example training in handling critical incidents and post-traumatic stress, if accidents or crime are potential hazards.

ISSUES IN EAP MANAGEMENT

To achieve a successful EAP programme, standard policies for programme administration, combined with clear-cut definitions of the programme's goals, need to be developed and maintained. In the following section, some of the relevant issues will be discussed in detail.

Confidentiality

The issue of confidentiality is vital. For an EAP to be well received and utilized, it must gain the employee's confidence that his or her privacy will be fully respected, irrespective of other company interests. This policy must be clearly stated and documented, with back-up from an active programme of education within the company to explain the issues and their importance. Often employees will voice fears that sensitive personal data will be revealed to management, and that management will make adverse use of this information. It is therefore helpful in the early stages of EAP implementation to indicate to employees the location of records (best placed with an external provider), the security with which they are stored, the fact that no one other than professional counselling staff has access to them, and the fact that EAP staff are bound by their professional code of ethics to ensure that appropriate standards of confidentiality are maintained. Management, on the other hand, even and perhaps especially if they are genuinely concerned about the welfare of employees, may not always recognize the importance of these issues. Therefore, it is important for the EAP professionals to draw clear boundaries for information exchange and to establish agreed guidelines with management.

Employee Counselling Today's (1992) special issue on confidentiality stated that 'If the boundaries of confidentiality are unclear all parties will be left with an interpretation which, at best, serves their own interests and, at worst, stupefies the counselling initiative... Consequently creating the right framework and establishing a sound level of understanding and acceptance are crucial.' It is apparent that matters of confidentiality within counselling are ethically and legally complex. Questions that arise include, for example: when is breaking confidentiality permissible or mandatory, who needs to know what and why, and how vulnerable is the counsellor if there are inconsistencies in the agreements on confidentiality? With regard to the first of these questions, the relevant professional codes of ethics make it clear that the one circumstance in which confidentiality may be breached is when failure to do so exposes others or clients themselves to serious risk of harm.

Issues of confidentiality can pose considerable difficulties for EAP counsellors, since employees need to know that their records are kept in confidence, while company managers want to have information by which to evaluate the effectiveness of both their workforce and the programme itself. The best way to guard against the conflicts inherent in this situation is to establish the precise terms on which confidentiality is guaranteed to the employees. Thus, a cohesive policy regarding confidentiality should be a major feature in any EAP.

EAP Staff Qualifications

As pointed out above, a variety of professional disciplines are usually represented in an EAP programme. Each contributes its own orientation and philosophy about human development and problem resolution. Educational level combined with clinical experience and, at times, personal recovery from problems are important indicators for an effective assessment and referral role. The ability accurately to assess the problem and to make appropriate referrals will determine the effective use of resources and have a major impact on optimum service delivery and treatment outcome.

Sonnenstuhl and Trice (1986) outline the following qualifications for an EAP coordinator or director: (i) strong understanding of organizational structures and processes, including human resource management and medical divisions; (ii) general understanding of the health and social service resources available to the employees; (iii) skills in administration and communication; and (iv) compassion for employees' problems. These researchers suggest that counselling experience may be helpful but not required. However, other specialists in the EAP field disagree, for instance stating that: 'Educational background should be at the doctoral level in psychology, psychiatry, or clinical social work. Staff members should certainly be skilled diagnosticians and practitioners of short-term group and individual psychotherapy' (Manuso, 1985).

Ultimately the issue of the appropriate staff qualifications will depend on the focus of the EAP programme, on whether for example the primary service aims are concerned with mental-health problems, with chemical dependence, or with resolving work-related problems. For a full-service programme (Jones, 1985; see above), it is essential that the delivery of clinical services is embedded into a properly constituted line of clinical responsibility; in the StressCare programme, this line extends right the way up to senior clinical staff within a major psychiatric teaching hospital. This line of clinical responsibility, however, needs to be paralleled by an administrative line, since it is wasteful of a highly qualified clinical resource if this is applied to administration (e.g. liaising with the company or its line management). This dual line of responsibility, in turn, requires very close coordination between the two. In the StressCare programme, for example, each counsellor is fully briefed with relevant information, held on a computer next to the telephone, about the company background, information that has been gathered by the administrative staff who liaise with the company's line management, personnel and medical departments.

The EAP staff also have to be skilled communicators and trainers. Effective implementation of an EAP depends critically upon the clarity of communication to the entire workforce; and effective liaison between the EAP provider and the company entails a considerable educational effort in keeping supervisory staff abreast of relevant new information and techniques. Clearly, given the range of these demands upon them, the EAP staff must themselves be highly trained, and so able to increase the visibility of the programme, gain credibility within the organisation, create better communications with the management, and improve relations with the employees.

Data Collection and Record Keeping

In order to establish a monitoring system which will eventually serve as the basis for programme evaluation, data collection and record keeping are further vital aspects of an EAP that need to be developed from the very earliest stages. Record keeping provides vital statistics in answering such questions as: 'Does the EAP have any effect?' and 'Why is it effective (or not)?'

The data collected may be divided into three categories. First, there are demographic characteristics: name of the employee, code number, age, sex, date of birth, etc. Second, there are forms that track the progress of referral and treatment: for example assessment, referral, case intake or termination forms. It is also useful to include a form which the employee can complete anonymously after the termination of counselling to determine how effective he or she found the treatment. Finally, there are job performance records: absenteeism, tardiness, unpredictable behaviour, conflicts with colleagues, morale, accidents, etc.

Roman and Blum (1985) maintain that successful EAPs that have managed to become an integral part of the organization have used record keeping as a tool to ensure their position. From their research, they give three reasons for record keeping: (i) record keeping is part of routine company procedures, and EAP programmes should also conform to the norm of information management within the organization; (ii) records facilitate the possibility of staff succession in the event of EAP staff turnover; and (iii) records are helpful in the development of management information. Information from the records may also provide indications as to the overall efficiency of the programme. However, the observant reader will have noticed that these considerations are likely in at least some instances to contradict the overriding need for confidentiality, discussed above. If, for example, absenteeism is to be correlated with attendance at counselling sessions, the gathering of the relevant data may inadvertently reveal to line management the names of individuals who have received counselling. Only very careful and detailed discussion with management of the appropriate procedures to follow, and strict adherence to them, can overcome these difficulties. Whatever procedures are agreed, they must leave information about individual treatment and treatment outcome exclusively in the hands of the clinicians concerned. Thus, on a number of key issues, management must usually be satisfied, in the interests of confidentiality, with only general statistical information.

As more companies implement EAPs, reliable methods for programme evaluation become increasingly necessary. While there is much disagreement as to the best ways to evaluate a programme, the first step is to gather reliable data so that at least some form of analysis is possible. Thus the issue of record keeping brings us naturally to the next issue: programme evaluation.

PROGRAMME EVALUATION

Descriptive surveys, anecdotal reports and individual programme evaluations frequently point to the success of EAPs. A number of studies have shown EAP interventions to be effective in terms of: the percentage of employees who take up the service; the extent to which employees who receive assistance improve in their job performance; the extent to which the employee responds positively to the assistance given; and savings in costs for the company. However, while this evidence for the positive effects of EAPs is encouraging, these same reports have also been the subject of much methodological criticism. Among the flaws most frequently mentioned are the lack of appropriate control groups (i.e.

groups of employees to whom the EAP is not provided, but who are in other respects comparable to those given access to the programme), and lack of objective measures (e.g. improvement in job performance, reduction in absenteeism). The first of these flaws is hard to overcome. Given that an EAP is perceived as an employee benefit, and indeed needs to be publicized as such in order to ensure proper take-up, it is extremely difficult if not impossible to withhold the service from a segment of the staff for the sake of conducting a scientific evaluation. (This, of course, is a familiar ethical problem that has received much attention in the context of controlled clinical trials of putative new medical therapies.) Thus, while the use of proper control groups is highly recommended, the opportunities to conduct evaluations of this kind in the workplace are rare indeed. The second flaw—lack of objective data—is in principle much easier to deal with. However, in our experience it is remarkably difficult to prise the relevant performance data out of the company's line managers. Thus, even when EAP providers are fully willing to cooperate with a hard-nosed evaluation of their enterprise, it is often necessary to fall back upon the softer data, concerned with clients' and therapists' perceptions of the outcome of counselling, that the providers themselves possess.

Even when management is willing to provide performance data, the choice of criteria and their appropriate interpretation provide further problems. Many companies do not have well developed performance measures. If they do have them, EAP evaluation requires that they be made available, not only for those who take up the programme, but also for those who do not. The latter data are necessary both to provide a benchmark against which to compare the performance of those who take up the service and as a further defence against a breach of confidentiality. Thus, even when only a small percentage of the workforce takes up the service, a considerable body of data has to be provided by the company, which may well balk at the amount of extra work therefore required. Another problem is that objective performance criteria have often been developed for only the lower echelons of the workforce. Yet it seems likely that improvements in mental health, consequent upon counselling, bring benefits to the company that are positively correlated with the size of the budget controlled by the individual counselled.

A further problem is that EAP staff frequently take on programme evaluation as one of their own roles. This is clearly inappropriate, since with the best will in the world it is hard to stand back and contemplate the possibility that one has been working to no effect. The company commissioning an EAP is also not well placed to conduct an evaluation, both because the staff normally lack the necessary training and skills and because, by the very act of commissioning an EAP, they too are predisposed to believe they have made the correct decision. The preferred solution, therefore, would be evaluation by a third party, but without additional investment this is not normally possible. (However, a study of just this kind has recently been commissioned by the UK Health and Safety Executive, and is being conducted by Professor C. L. Cooper's group. When they become available, the results of this study should be particularly informative.) In the absence of an appropriate third party, the next best solution is for the company and EAP provider jointly to conduct an evaluation, each scrutinizing the quality of the data provided by the other.

Most of the existing data supporting the effectiveness of EAPs can be challenged on one or all of the above methodological grounds. However, while it is essential to remain aware of these potential pitfalls, it is also important to realize that, from a more pragmatic point of view, service consumers (employees), sponsors (employers) and providers (EAP staff) generally express high levels of satisfaction with these programmes. The increasing prevalence of EAPs among work organizations is an indication of this general level of satisfaction. Thus, as documented by EAPA (1992a), (i) the 1991 National Executive Poll on Health Care Costs and Benefits showed that 68% of the responding organizations offered EAPs; (ii) in a survey of 5786 employers by Tilinghast (a management consulting firm), 57% of employers reported offering an EAP as a way of containing health costs; and (iii) a survey of 578 human resource executives by the Olsten Corporation showed that 65% of responding companies offered drug and alcohol abuse programmes.

A review of a range of studies led McGowan (1984) to conclude that occupational programmes, including EAPs, are highly successful once identification of cases and referral have taken place, and that evidence of this success can be found in improved job performance. For example, in one study of effectiveness, the Orange County (Florida) Public Schools demonstrated that intervention through their EAP significantly reduced long-term sick leave and medical benefit claims among their staff. Employees who first contacted the EAP in 1986 took nearly 14 fewer sick leaves in 1991 than the average for non-EAP users. This result suggests that an EAP intervention may produce long-term as well as immediate benefits (EAPA, 1992a).

In terms of cost-effectiveness, the US Department of Labor (1990) reported that employers generally find that, for every $1 invested in an EAP, savings of $5 to as much as $16 are achieved. In one of the most comprehensive studies of this kind, the McDonnell Douglas Corporation reported that, over the years 1985–1989, for every $1 spent on their EAP, they saved $5, with a net saving of $3.8 million in 1989. The bulk of the savings (85%) were due to a decrease in medical claims (EAPA, 1992a). This estimate of savings is, in fact, conservative, since it takes no account of potential additional costs (for replacement, recruitment, training, etc.) in respect of those individuals who, but for the help received via the EAP, might have left the company prematurely. One of the reasons for the high cost-effectiveness of EAPs is that they are surprisingly inexpensive. The StressCare programme, described above, for example can usually be provided for less than £20 per family per annum (the actual cost depending inversely upon the size of the workforce covered). Given the enormous overall economic burden associated with psychological distress and stress-related illness, this evidence for the cost-effectiveness of EAPs, if reliable, suggests that their widespread use might lead to very considerable savings at a national level.

Consider, as an example, substance abuse. Drug and alcohol abuse give rise to costs for companies in terms of direct treatment, morbidity, reduced or lost productivity and mortality costs. The cost of alcoholism and related problems in the United States was estimated to be $85.8 billion in 1988. In this estimate, 39% is attributed to reduced productivity, and 33% to mortality loss (Rice, Kelman, Miller and Dunmeyer, 1988). The relationships between alcohol use and a variety of diseases and disorders are well documented. For example, alcohol is involved in 53% of all motorway deaths, 50% of spouse abuse, 38% of child abuse, and 54% of incarcerations for violent crimes (EAPA, 1992b). Of 265 respondents to a survey by *Fortune* magazine, a large number indicated that substance abuse led to 'a significant or very significant' increase in medical benefits (74%); to increased absenteeism (67%); to decreased productivity (64%); or to more disciplinary proceedings (44%) (EAPA, 1992b).

That is the debit side. On the credit side, there is evidence that EAPs can have a beneficial effect on this huge problem. Thus, in a study conducted at Harvard and Boston University, it was shown that alcoholics identified by an EAP have a better chance of recovery. The data showed that alcoholics attending a hospital-based treatment and AA relapsed only 23% of the time, as compared to those choosing their own treatment, who relapsed 38% of the time, and those attending only AA, who relapsed 63% of the time (Walsh, Hingson, Merrigan et al., 1991). Commenting on this study, Goodwin (1991) noted that the record for outpatient treatment of alcoholism, of a kind that has frequently been offered by EAPs, has in fact usually been superior to the results obtained by Walsh et al. For example, Trice and Beyer (1984) investigated an EAP programme in a major American corporation with 120 000 employees in order to evaluate the effectiveness of various psycho-therapeutic approaches, including constructive confrontation and counselling. The data were collected from two samples of supervisors (n = 474) who had a subordinate with a drinking problem referred to the EAP programme, or a subordinate who presented other behavioural problems. The results showed that 75% of the problem drinkers and 55% of other troubled employees showed a marked improvement in their performance after having been confronted and referred to the EAP programme. The authors concluded that constructive confrontations motivated employees to change their behaviour, while counselling offered them one means of doing so.

Given the recent appearance of EAPs on the British scene, it is not surprising that there are far fewer data concerning their effectiveness in this country. It seems clear enough, however, that the scale of the problems that EAPs are intended to address is similar on both sides of the Atlantic. Thus, the Confederation of British Industry (1993) concluded that work-related stress is the number one factor causing absenteeism in the UK. Increased competition, rapid job obsolescence, the repeated need for job retraining, difficulties in balancing demands from work and family, and enforced redundancy are among the many reasons why workers and their families are today experiencing an increased level of stress. Stress has become, in the 1990s, one of the most important occupational health issues facing business in the UK. While many researchers are investigating the causes and consequences of stress, companies bear the cost of the effects of stress in the form of increased work-related accident rates, sickness absence, inefficiency, premature death, and staff turnover (Goodman, 1991). The importance of stress is reflected in a British Heart Foundation study (cited in Cooper et al., 1990) which estimated that heart disease alone costs a company of 1000 employees £200 000 a year. This figure is based on the assumption that 5700 working days are lost and 4.6 workers die prematurely in each such company. In total, heart disease costs British industry £1.5 billion p.a. in lost working days. Over 2 million people in the UK suffer from illness which they believe is caused, or made worse, by their work. An annual total of about 29 million days off work is reported as being due to work-related injuries and ill health (Health and Safety Executive, 1991).

The problems, then, are the same in the UK and the USA; what of the remedy? There is no reason to suppose that the nature of stress, the psychological and psycho-physiological responses to stress, or the effectiveness of psychological treatments for the resulting conditions differ between the two sides of the Atlantic. Indeed, many of the most effective psychological and counselling techniques for dealing with emotional problems were first developed in Britain and then exported to the USA (Watts, 1985, 1988; Hackman, 1993). However, the financial and regulatory background against which mental ill health affects performance at work differs markedly between the two countries. In particular, in the United States relative to the United Kingdom, business bears a far greater share of the costs of medical care, and both insurance companies and the legal system give much greater recognition to the reality of psychological influences upon health and performance. Thus, any amelioration of the adverse effects of mental ill health upon physical health and performance at work has a much greater influence upon an American balance-sheet (in the form, e.g. of reduced health insurance premiums) than upon a British one. Nonetheless, there are other savings which would be expected to occur equally in both settings, especially those that directly reflect performance at work (e.g. absenteeism due to sickness; staff turnover and consequent increased recruitment and training costs).

There is so far only one published British study against which to test this expectation. The Post Office began a pilot project offering an in-house counselling service to its staff in 1986. Several evaluations were conducted to assess the effectiveness of this service using pre- and post-treatment data (based on 188 experimental subjects and 100 random controls) concerned with sickness absence, mental health, self-esteem, organizational commitment and changes in behaviour related to health (Cooper and Sadri, 1991). The results showed that, at the completion of counselling, employees were less anxious (62%), suffered fewer psychosomatic symptoms (61%), were less depressed (60%) and had higher self-esteem. In addition, six months after counselling, a significant fall in the number of absences was reported: there was a 27% improvement in absence events and a 22% improvement in days lost, while controls showed no significant difference in scores over the same period of time. Thus, the Post Office study suggests that, in the UK as in the USA, intervention can lead to a healthier workforce, which in turn should lead to a healthier organization.

FUTURE RESEARCH

EAPs are now spreading rapidly in Britain. It is therefore becoming urgent to have additional, properly controlled investigations of their effectiveness and cost-effectiveness so as to supplement the meagre data base provided at present by the Post Office study described in the previous section. In setting up such investigations, certain points should be borne in mind.

First, it is necessary to define clearly the measures that will be used in evaluating the success of the EAP. In doing so, it is important not to confuse mere record keeping (see the section above) with programme evaluation. It should also be noted that it is impossible, from a practical point of view, to collect data on every conceivable measure; what distinguishes a well-planned evaluation is a clear definition at the outset of the outcome measures to be collected. Steps that need to be undertaken in achieving such a definition include the following.

1 Clarify the scope of the EAP service and determine what elements, in consequence, are most pertinent to the evaluation. Identified variables must have explicitly defined parameters and characteristics, and be capable of being quantified.
2 Determine how change is to be measured, e.g. by:

   (a) *Problematic behaviour*—the degree to which the person succeeds in controlling or eliminating the behaviour;
   (b) *Work performance*—improved job performance, morale, coworker/supervisory relations, absenteeism, accidents;
   (c) *Cost reduction*—savings from improved work performance, staff turnover, tardiness, benefit claims, sickness, overtime costs, average cost of training an employee;
   (d) *Utility*—number of employees serviced by the programme, type of problem for which assistance was sought, source of referral.

3 Develop reliable and valid measures of these kinds of change.
4 Identify who is responsible for the analysis and interpretation of the results. Many studies can be improved by involving external experts who will objectively interpret the result.

Wider acceptance of EAP programmes will come only when their effects have been substantiated by research. As EAPs become more established, future programmes should endeavour to integrate research into practice. Unfortunately, few companies have either the time or the inclination to develop long-term research. However, academic institutions are increasingly taking the initiative in linking up with the business community in order to examine the effectiveness of counselling in the workplace. Collaboration of this kind is vital if good research is to be translated into better practice.

REFERENCES

Brandes, S. D. (1970). *American Welfare Capitalism*. Chicago: University of Chicago Press.

Confederation of British Industry (1993). *Too much time out? CBI/Percom survey on absence from work*. London: CBI.

Cooper, C. & Sadri, G. (1991). The impact of stress counselling at work. *Handbook on Job Stress* (Special Issue). *Journal of Social Behaviour & Personality*, **6**, 4411–4423.

Cooper, C., Sadri, G., Allison, T. & Reynolds, P. (1990). Stress counselling in the Post Office. *Counselling Psychology Quarterly*, **3**, 3–11.

Dobson, K. S. (1989). A meta-analysis of the efficacy of cognitive therapy for depression. *Journal of Consulting and Clinical Psychology*, **22**, 326–330.

Employee Assistance Professionals Association, Inc. (1990). *EAPA Professional Program Standards*, Arlington, Virginia.

Employee Assistance Professionals Association, Inc. (1992a). *EAPA Press File: EAP Utilization and Cost Benefits*, Arlington, Virginia.

Employee Assistance Professionals Association, Inc. (1992b). *EAPA Press File: Alcoholism and other Drug Abuse in America and its Workplace*. Arlington, Virginia.

Employee Counselling Today, (1992). Special Issue No. 4: Confidentiality and Ethics.

Erfurt, J. C. & Foote, A. (1985). Variations in EAP programs, In S. H. Klarreich, J. L. Francek and C. E. Moore (eds), *The Human Resource Management Handbook*. New York: Praeger, pp. 45–58.

Goodman, S. (1991). A solution to stress. *Journal of the American Chamber of Commerce (UK)*, 10–11 September.

Goodwin, D. W. (1991). Inpatient treatment of alcoholism—new life for the Minneapolis plan. *New England Journal of Medicine*, **325**, 804–806.

Hackman, A. (1993). Behavioural and cognitive psychotherapies: past history, current applications and future registration issues. *Behavioural and Cognitive Psychotherapy*, Supplement 1.

Health and Safety Executive (1991). *The HSE Annual Report 1990–91*. London: HMSO.

Jones, O. F. (1985) The rationale and critical issues of EAP development. In S. H. Klarreich, J. L. Francek and C. E. Moore (eds), *The Human Resource Management Handbook*. New York: Praeger, pp. 7–13.

McGowan, B. G. (1984). *Trends in Employee Counselling Programs*. New York: Pergamon Press.

Manuso, J. J. (1985). Occupational clinical psychologist. In S. H. Klarreich, J. L. Francek and C. E. Moore (eds), *The Human Resource Management Handbook*. New York: Praeger, pp. 155–163.

Marks, I. M. (1987). *Fears, Phobias and Rituals: Panic, Anxiety and Their Disorders*. New York: Oxford University Press.

Mayo, E. (1923). Irrationality and reverie. *Journal of Personnel Research*, **1**, 477–483.

Presnell, L. F. (1981). *Occupational Counselling and Referral Systems*. Salt Lake City: Utah Alcoholism Foundation.

Rice, D., Kelman, S., Miller, L. & Dunmeyer, S. (1988). The economic costs of alcohol and drug abuse and mental illness. Office of Financing and Coverage Policy of the Alcohol, Drug Abuse and Mental Health Administration.

Roman, P. M. & Blum T. C. (1985). Models and levels of data management affecting the EAP practitioner, In S. H. Klarreich, J. L. Francek and C. E. Moore (eds), *The Human Resource Management Handbook*. New York: Praeger, pp. 203–222.

Sonnenstuhl, W. J. & Trice, H. M. (1986). *Strategies for Employee Assistance Programs: The Crucial Balance*. New York: ILR Press.

Trice, H. M. & Beyer, J. (1984). Work-related outcomes of constructive confrontation strategies in a job-based alcoholism program. *Journal of Studies on Alcohol*, **45**, 393–404.

Trice, H. M. & Schonbrunn, M. (1981). A history of job-based alcoholism programs 1900–1955. *Journal of Drug Issues*, **11**, 171–198.

US Department of Labor (1990). *What Works: Workplaces without Drugs*. Washington DC, 17.

Walsh, D. C., Hingson, R. W., Merrigan, D. M., Levenson, S. M., Cupples, A., Heeren, T., Coffman, G. A., Becker, C. A., Barker, T. A., Hamilton, S. K., McGuire, T. G. & Kelly, C. A. (1991). A randomized trial of treatment options for alcohol-abusing workers. *New England Journal of Medicine*, **325**, 775–782.

Watts, F. N. (ed.) (1985, 1988). *New Developments in Clinical Psychology*, Vols 1 and 2. Chichester: British Psychological Society and Wiley.

12
Conclusions to Creating Healthy Work Organizations

CARY L. COOPER AND STEPHEN WILLIAMS

The previous chapters have given a comprehensive, practical guide to ways of creating healthy organizations. They have shown that successful programmes to improve employee health are carefully planned, effectively implemented and properly evaluated. We can all improve the health of our employees by implementing some of the principles and techniques described in this book. It is not necessary to try to do everything at once, and the case studies should be seen as models of 'good practice' that can be used as a blueprint for action and implemented in stages.

The following checklist (Table 12.1) describes some of the characteristics of healthy organizations. The list is by no means exhaustive, but gives an indication of some of the attributes of organizational health.

In many ways, the move towards creating healthy work organizations is similar to the development of the quality movement. It is only in the last couple of decades that quality has become an important issue in Western organizations. Traditionally, quality was the responsibility of quality inspectors who checked other people's work and dealt with

Creating Healthy Work Organizations. Edited by C. L. Cooper and S. Williams.
© 1994 John Wiley & Sons Ltd

Table 12.1   *A checklist of organizational health*

Tick list (✔)	Characteristics
	Environmental
☐	The Health and Safety regulations are fully observed.
☐	Work place hazards are monitored.
☐	Employees follow good environmental and ergonomic practices.
☐	The working environment is as pleasant as the work processes allow.
	Physical
☐	Health screening programmes are available.
☐	The organization runs health education programmes.
☐	There are facilities for exercise.
☐	Healthy eating is encouraged.
	Mental
☐	Employees can discuss their problems in confidence at work.
☐	Communications are open and frequent, and managers practise active listening.
☐	Morale is high.
	Social
☐	There is mutual respect between managers and staff.
☐	The organization has flexible working and flexible benefit systems.
☐	Employees look forward to coming to work.

failures. The role of occupational health followed a similar pattern. The company doctor or nurse dealt with accidents and illness, and played a remedial rather than preventive role in the health of the workforce. The quality movement took off when organizations began to realize the cost of non-conformance and the necessity of dealing with problems at their source. It seems obvious now that it is more efficient and effective to build 'quality' into the beginning of a process than to spend time dealing with the rejects at the end. However, many organizations still believe that health care should be remedial. They fail to understand the benefits of improving the well-being of the healthy, and concentrate exclusively on the sick. Prevention is better than cure, and the most effective way to create a healthy organization is to practise the principles of primary healthcare to prevent illness from occurring.

The basic principles of the quality movement can be adapted for healthy organizations:

- Good health is everyone's responsibility
- Health promotion starts at the top
- Good health is about getting it right first time

Healthy organizations are quality organizations. A healthy organization really believes that people are its most important asset and does everything it can to promote their well-being. As people become more aware of the need to actively manage their health, the expectations of the services provided by their employers will continue to increase. The demands of employees for better health programmes will be matched by the growing recognition of the financial benefits of good health. Organizations rarely act for altruistic reasons, and need to understand the relationship between a healthy workforce and success. Good healthcare programmes are about striving for excellence; they are not about avoiding problems. Action to improve organizational health will lead to a more creative, committed, enthusiastic and involved workforce. We can all get better at promoting good health, and the organizations featured in this book are continuing to review and develop their programmes. Their experiences have been of significant benefit to many thousands of employees, and we hope they will encourage other organizations to develop effective ways of enhancing the health of their staff.

Index

Index compiled by Caroline Sheard